You Want Me to Do What?

ELIZABETH L. SMOOT

YOU WANT ME TO DO WHAT?

A Devotional for Stay-at-Home Moms

(or Those Who Would Like to Be)

CLC PUBLICATIONS
FORT WASHINGTON, PENNSYLVANIA 19034

Published by CLC Publications

U.S.A.
P.O. Box 1449, Fort Washington, PA 19034

GREAT BRITAIN
51 The Dean, Alresford, Hants. SO24 9BJ

AUSTRALIA
P.O. Box 419M, Manunda, QLD 4879

NEW ZEALAND
10 MacArthur Street, Feilding

ISBN 0-87508-637-3

Copyright © 2000
Elizabeth L. Smoot

Cover design: *Skip Mable Studio*

This printing 2001

Printed in the United States of America

Contents

Chapter	Page
Preface	7
1. You Want Me to Do What? *Fear, Worry*	9
2. Exhibition Round *Complimenting Yourself*	17
3. Hands *Resting in God's Hands*	23
4. Don't Forget the Sabbath *The 4th Commandment*	31
5. Thank You for the Gift *Spiritual Gifts*	43
6. Ones, Twos and Threes *Accepting Our Children*	51
7. Becoming a Kingdom Bookworm *Christian Literature*	57
8. Ruth *Women of the Bible*	67
9. Wanted: Spelunkers - Apply Within *A Deeper Relationship with Jesus*	77
10. Am I Bearing Fruit or Am I Just Fruity? *Serving and Fruits of the Spirit*	83
11. Patience *Saul*	91
12. Curtains *An Approachable God*	97
13. Out of Booties and Into Boot Camp! *Discipline/Training*	105
14. A Splash of Transformation *Reflecting Christ*	117
15. A Workout *Exercise*	125
16. Thankful Hearts *Being Thankful*	133
17. Do You Fall for the Mall? *Materialism*	139
18. Moving *Sin*	147
19. Lookin' Forward To Bein' Shucked! *Irritations/Strength*	153
20. Mittens *Reward*	163
21. Praying on Holy Ground *Prayer*	169
22. A Precious Seedling *The Responsibility of Children*	179
23. Going to the Chapel *Marriage*	185
24. The Reason for My Hope *Witnessing*	197
25. You'll Have a New Name *Overcoming and the Names of God*	205
26. The Filing Cabinet *Strangers*	211
27. Some Final Thoughts	221

Acknowledgments

My deepest appreciation to:

... My best friend and husband, Rob. Thank you for your support and love. Even when we were struggling financially, you've always supported my decision to be a stay-at-home mom.

... Our three beautiful children, Brielle, Brandy and Hunter. Thank you for changing my life. I pray that you may know the greatest joy, which is being a parent.

... My parents, grandparents, father- and mother-in-law and family. Thank you for your support and kindness. I am very blessed.

... The Swisher family. Thank you for letting me tag along and attend church with your family.

... Dr. David Bird. Thank you for teaching teachers.

... My friends. Thank you for your encouragement, love and prayers throughout this project.

... Mr. Richard Brodhag, Mr. Robert Delancy and others at CLC Publications for believing in this book.

Preface

YOU'LL quickly discover by reading this book that I'm not a writer. I'm a mom and a teacher. When the Lord put a burden on my heart to write this book for Stay-at-Home Mothers, I quickly reminded Him that I was the one who had big red "RE DO"s at the top of all of her English Composition papers. This book proves that God can and will use very ordinary people.

Now that this book has traveled from the bookshelf to your hands, I'll repeat the prayer I prayed when I mailed the first two chapters away to potential publishers: "Lord, I pray that, although I am not a seasoned writer, moms will see my heart. Let me share the good news of Jesus. And may my meanderings somehow end up at the cross and point them to the One who put this deep love for children in their hearts in the first place."

I want this book to encourage you as you stay at home and mold children for eternity. The career of motherhood is the most important career. I want to uplift you. You may be in the "season" of your life right now when you want just to be a mother. That is okay. In fact, it is fantastic! Don't listen to the world. Listen to your heart. God will honor you for your time, your countless sacrifices, and your true commitment.

Each chapter of this book tells a short story and gives a practical application of scripture from the Bible. Many mothers love the Lord and want to read the Word, yet they struggle to understand the Bible or see how it applies to their everyday lives. I hope this book will show you that the Bible is the source of Living Water. Once you discover that, you'll find yourself going to God's Word every day for wisdom, refreshment and hope. It does have something to say to what we, as mothers, are going through.

The second part of each chapter is a prayer. I hope that you'll jump-start your prayer life. You have a heavenly Father who wants to help you and be with you through all of the ups and downs of motherhood.

The third section of each chapter presents an early childhood activity that you can do with your children. Sometimes it will be an activity to help prepare your child for school, while other chapters are devoted to activities and discussions that will foster your child's relationship with Jesus.

Years from now, no one will remember what kind of house you had, what car you drove, or the clothes you wore. What *will* remain will be your *children*. Bless you for putting them first! Know that your efforts will be remembered in their lives and by future generations.

A very wise person once said, "True Christianity is not saying to others, 'Here . . . you must believe this, do this, and think this . . . .' True Christianity is one poor, hungry beggar showing another poor, hungry beggar where he found some bread." May Christ get the glory as fresh bread crumbs are sprinkled throughout each chapter of my book.

At the top of each chapter page you'll see a little picture or code. I've coded my chapters according to their length. I recognize that every day is different: some days you'll have a small block of time for reading and other days a larger block of time.

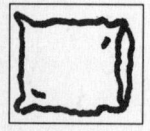

The pillow does not mean that I think you'll be bored with this chapter and consequently fall asleep. The pillow means that this is a *short chapter*. It's short enough to read in bed before your few precious hours of sleep.

The teacup lets you know that this is a chapter of *medium* length. It could be finished by the time you get to the very last drop of a nice hot cup of tea.

The sleeping baby denotes the *longer* chapters. I invite you to curl up somewhere while your little ones are napping. I'll be saying a prayer that you'll finish the chapter and have a quiet Bible study with the Lord before those little eyes open again.

Chapter 1

Fear, Worry

1

You Want Me to Do What?

Mary: "You want me to tell Joseph *what*?"
Moses: "Take this staff and do *what*?"
Joshua: "Walk around Jericho seven times and blow *what*?"
David: "Take this little stone and slingshot and do *what*?"

*D*O YOU ever wonder what you've gotten yourself into now that you've decided to be a stay-at-home mom? Do you feel strong and bold some days, yet inadequate on other days? Are you fearful that you don't have the ability to be the kind of mother you want to be? Does the task of rearing your children, caring for your home, keeping your body in some sort of shape, staying friend and lover with your husband, and nourishing your own mind and spirit during these "stay-at-home" years seem like a job from MISSION IMPOSSIBLE? Do you feel like *you* may self-destruct instead of the *message* doing so? Well, if you're shaking your head yes, you are not alone. But don't make excuses and say that you can't do it. You can!

Let's look in the Bible's book of Judges, chapters 6 and 7, where we meet a man named Gideon. This man also faced an overwhelming task. He tried to give excuses to God. God, however, promised Gideon that He would give him all the tools and support he would need to be successful. Gideon was *so* unsure of himself. He kept asking God to give him signs instead of simply trusting the peace he felt inside concerning God's will. God wanted Gideon to put his trust in *Him*, not in what was going on around him or what made sense to the natural man. Once Gideon was convinced that God was walking beside him, he began to obey with power and strength!

Are you haunted by questions? "What if I get lonely being a stay-at-home mom? I'll be the only tall person in the house all day! What if we can't pay the bills on one salary? What if I lose control and gain tons of weight? What will I feel like when all of my friends get promotions, have great salaries, and go on those nice vacations? What if I begin to lose myself in the lives of my children? What if my husband doesn't find me as attractive or exciting as he use to? What if? What if? What if?" Fears. Doubts. Worries. These are not from God. Satan wants you to feel fear, to distrust God and question yourself. God wants you to confront these doubts and fears, believe in Him, and step out. He is ready and willing to help you with each concern that you may have.

Staying at home and committing yourself to motherhood is a job that you, with God's help, are equipped to do. The pay is horrible. The satisfaction is awesome. Will it always be easy? Definitely not. Wonderful things are rarely easy. But God teaches us through trials and tests. You are in a time of sowing. Hang on. The reaping will come. You'll be so thankful for the choices and sacrifices you made. Approach these years as testing times, as not losing yourself but finding yourself. God wants to be your strength.

Look at the beginning of this chapter. You don't think Mary, Moses, Joshua and David from the Bible ever felt fear? Of course they did! But they were determined. They each demonstrated great faith and love for a God they could not see but who was indeed *real* to them in their hearts and in their past experiences.

The choices we make affect many things. Many people *say* that relationships are more important than things, but do their lives show it? Relationships take time. You are giving up time now to nurture your children. You are investing in your family's future—perhaps not the future of your bank account, but the future of your relationship with your kids. Working hard to acquire *things* will not bring happiness. Our culture is finding this out the hard way. Those things are just that: *Things! People* matter. *Children* matter.

Life's experiences count for something if they are built on a strong foundation. God has already promised us in His Word to supply all that we need. I have been a stay-at-home mom for many years and I can say that God has always provided everything I've needed. I didn't say He provided everything I *wanted*. God pours the foundation (His Word and His promises to us His children), then He backs up the truck and supplies what we need. It's my job to pick up the tool belt, strap it around me, and get busy (with my husband) building my home. Oh, I'll be honest, there were months when I thought God's supply truck had forgotten my address, but He never did. There were times when I was hoping He would deliver some new clothes or petty cash. He decided to drop off loads of imagination and thankfulness instead.

Don't say, "You want me to do WHAT for the next few years?" Instead say, "God, I can't WAIT to see what You and I are going to do with this little family of mine!"

Scripture to meditate on today:

Ephesians 1:18–21 (TLB)
I pray that your hearts will be flooded with light so that you can see something of the future he has called you to share. I want you to realize that God has been made rich because we who are Christ's have been given to him! I pray that you will begin to understand how incredibly great his power is to help those who believe him. It is that same mighty power that raised Christ from the dead and seated him in the place of honor at God's right hand in heaven.

✦ A mother's response: I'll get my help and power from God. Free refills!

• • • • •

Colossians 3:2 (TLB)
Let heaven fill your thoughts; don't spend your time worrying about things down here. You should have as little desire for this world as a dead person does. Your real life is in heaven with Christ and God.

✦ What troubles? God and I can handle this stuff. I'm only passing through!

• • • • •

Colossians 2:7 (TLB)

Let your roots grow down into him and draw up nourishment from him. See that you go on growing in the Lord, and become strong and vigorous in the truth.

◆ What burnout? Winds of trials will blow against me, but my roots are so deep I'll bend, but I won't break! Yes, you are stronger than you think!

• • • • •

1 Timothy 6:6–7 (TLB)

Do you want to be truly rich? You already are if you are happy and good. After all, we didn't bring any money with us when we came into the world, and we can't carry away a single penny when we die.

◆ What jealousy? I'm rich in all the important things. And so are you! Instead of striving for deeper pockets, I'll strive for deeper relationships with my children, my husband, and my Creator.

• • • • •

Isaiah 45:2 (TLB)

I will go before you, Cyrus, and level the mountains and smash down the city gates of brass and iron bars. And I will give you treasures hidden in the darkness, secret riches; and you will know that I am doing this—I, the Lord, the God of Israel, the one who calls you by your name.

◆ What obstacles? My God goes before me in every situation and helps me. God knows my name! My treasure box is filled with children's laughter, and my own tears of joy for the privilege of being a mother.

Prayer of the Day

Heavenly Father,

I don't want to be controlled by the spirits of fear and worry. You know I have lots of questions, Lord. But I refuse to run from hard things. You've shown me in the past that the things that take hard work are always the best things. Help me to believe in myself and the abilities that You have given me. Help me to rise to the challenge of being at home with this little family. Give me eyes of optimism. Give me courage, boldness, and a pioneering heart and mind. I'll remember that to get my harvest I must first enter a time of planting... to build something beautiful I must first start with a strong foundation. Jesus, I'll hold the nail while You grab the hammer. And I won't worry about my thumb. Amen.

Early Childhood Tip

To stick with our WHAT? theme today, I invite you to play the game "What's Missing?" with your child. This is a great game to help your child with visual memory— an important prereading skill. Get a tray and three small household items. For example: place a spoon, a cup, and scissors on a tray. The items should be placed in a line with some space between them. Tell your child to look carefully at the items for a minute or two. Now tell your child to turn around and close his (or her) eyes. While Johnny is turned away, remove one item from the tray. Invite him to turn around and open his eyes. Ask, "What is missing?" If he can't remember, show him the item that you took and put it back on the tray, remembering to return it to its original position. Say, "Look at the tray carefully; there is a spoon, a cup, and scissors." Point to each item as you name it. Repeat the process and let him try again to identify the missing item.

Once the child has mastered three items, move up to four and even five items. Go slowly—this may take months. Don't overwhelm.

This game trains the eye to remember shapes and order. This game will, in a concrete way, train your little one's eyes so that when they meet the abstract letters (ABC's) they'll be able to distinguish word patterns like *brat* and *rat*, *is* and *his*, and *do* and *dot*. (Did you notice that, although the pairs of words are similar, a letter is missing?) If children have practice in looking for differences—things that are missing—it will visually carry over to reading. The bonus is they think it's just a really fun game!

Here are some examples of other items you could put on the tray. (See, you knew that junk drawer would come in handy one day!) Three items: a fork, a pen, a small toy. Four items: a paper clip, a penny, a ring, a piece of candy. Five items: a spoon, a salt shaker, a crayon, a cup, and a clothespin.

Chapter 2

Complimenting Yourself

2

Exhibition Round

IT IS 3:00 p.m. on a clear, crisp winter day. Dinner is ready—check! Fuzzy slippers on—check! Tea simmering in my favorite mug—check! Family warned about the "no talking zone"—check! TV control in hand—check! Okay, I'm ready. I've been waiting for this day for a long time. Figure skating season begins today!

I've been a figure skating fan ever since I was a little girl. My mother would take me to see the Ice Capades every winter in the "sweetest town in the world"—Hershey, Pennsylvania. I'll never forget the first time I saw Peggy Fleming. She looked so beautiful, like a graceful butterfly on ice skates! She was a young woman then. Now she is a seasoned commentator for the sport. (I'm so relieved that the TV executives have finally figured out that women truly enjoy the sport.) I love everything about these winter games: the beautiful costumes, the enchanting music, the fluid body positions of the skaters. But the ice is hard, just like the rules and the pressure. During the competitions, the skaters strive to be perfect. The judges stare out coldly, looking for every mistake. Some of the commentators are ruthless in how they interpret the dance. You can see the strain on the athletes' faces. You can watch them pace at the sideboard and wipe their sweaty palms on the skirt of their lovely costume.

On the other hand, have you ever watched the exhibition rounds? Wacky fans like me will know instantly to what I'm referring. The exhibition rounds are held after the competition rounds. During these rounds, the skaters skate for fun—for themselves and for the audience. The performance is not judged, only enjoyed. These are my favorite performances because these are the best. The athletes are relaxed. They are free to enjoy the music and the rush of the wind as they glide around the ice and twirl into space. They almost always smile during the exhibition—rarely during the competition. They were too busy worrying what the judges, coaches, and other competitors were thinking to do such a thing as smile. The best way to describe it now is "they seem to be free." Do you know something I've discovered over the years of watching this winter sport? The skaters ordinarily don't fall during the exhibition time. The pressure isn't there and they don't stumble. On the rare occasion when they do fall, they quickly pick themselves up, shrug their shoulders, and skate on as if nothing ever happened.

We stay-at-home moms always seem to think we're in the competition round. But I'm here to tell you—and somehow make you believe—that God has us moms entered in the *exhibition* rounds. We worry whether we can cope with the big job of staying home and surviving. It will be harder than training for any sports competition! "Was I graceful and trim enough? What are the other 'skaters' wearing? What are their routines like?" Do we compare ourselves to other moms in the play group or car pool? "My jumps aren't high enough, are they? Did I let anyone down?" Satan regularly puts pressure on us to perform! We need, however, to be able to live without fear of change or of other people's judgments! You made a decision to be a stay-at-home mom. You *can* do this, and you *will* do this well!

Yes, God wants you to enjoy these stay-at-home years. If you let Him, He will do a great work in you.

When you were working full-time, you received encouragement and recognition for the kind of performance you did. This helped you to work even harder—to push yourself, and to feel good about yourself. Now you've decided to stay home and raise your children. Everything is going to change. Your body is going to change with each and every pregnancy. Your finances are going to change as you learn to budget and live on one salary. Your marriage is going to change as the children and pressures eat away at your time together. Your friends may change as you and your family grow. Your house is going to change as it becomes a home for little people. Accepting these changes can be hard. You must now learn to compliment yourself, because no one else will. When I was an elementary school teacher, I enjoyed receiving compliments from my students' parents and my colleagues. Then I became a full-time mom. No one was at my house saying, "Liz, what a great job you did on folding that laundry." "Liz, excellent technique in bed making!" "Wow, I love the way you disciplined today." My point is, you are going to have to start complimenting *yourself*.

There were days when I felt I did not accomplish one thing. In fact, in the evenings, after putting the kids in bed and nursing the baby, I was sure that not only did I not accomplish anything that day, I was worse off than the day before! God helped me get through those times by assuring me that even though I felt alone, I was not alone; God would help me. I felt overwhelmed by all the things I had to do, and especially the new task of motherhood. I was—no, I still *am*—in over my head. But all this is not over God's head! He presses me so that I lean on Him more. It's the same for you. Every day, start with a list of things you would like to accomplish. Be realistic. As you finish each task, check it off. At the end of the day, look at your list and compliment yourself on all the things you did. It is a visual reminder that even though it looks like my life and home are in chaos, I did do something today. You won't become discouraged if you can see that you actually did make some progress. Don't worry if some jobs are incomplete and must be carried over to tomorrow. Believe in yourself! You have a great desire in your heart to be a wonderful (not perfect) mother. God gave you that dream. Don't you think He will be with you every step of the way to see you to the finish line?

In the Old Testament, Numbers 9:15–23, we find a story about the Israelites following the great cloud above the tabernacle. The cloud was the visual presence of God. When the cloud moved, they would move with it. The people traveled and camped wherever the cloud led them. Sometimes the cloud would remain in one place for months. Other times, it would move daily. Talk about having to be ready to move and change! They trusted, followed, and changed—knowing God was in control. They could see the cloud. Ask God, How can I be used here—*right now*—where You have placed me?

Be willing to let Him change things. Accept the change and the challenges that come with it. Be able to move to different levels and stages within yourself, both in your marriage and your relationships with your children. God will be the constant. You need to be grounded in the Lord. We are not to be grounded in our salaries, job titles, or social groups. Don't look to other sources for your recognition. That is what the *world* does. Go to God for your recognition. *He* sees you sacrificing to be the mother you are.

Compliment yourself, daily, so that you will not become discouraged. 1 Peter 1:6 says, "So be truly glad! There is wonderful joy ahead, even though the going is rough for a while down here" (TLB). You might want to put that one on an index card and tape it to the refrigerator!

Didn't you hear your name called? I did. *He* called your name. He wants you down on the ice for the exhibition round. It is *your* time. Now remember, relax and enjoy yourself. Take it one move, one spin, one jump at a time. Of course, you'll need to stay in the rink. It is your boundary: don't go out of the rink. Your wonderful blades only work on God's *ice*. If you go into the stands, you will surely trip—for the blades don't glide on the carpet in the aisles. You'll be protected in the *rink*. If you need to, hold onto the walls along the side. They are placed there for you. And someone will be shining a spotlight on you. It will be disconcerting at first, but you'll grow to understand its importance. The light will illuminate the ice directly in front of you, yet you will not be able to see the ice up ahead. So just trust. The ice, of course, is "slippy" and cold, and the rink is dark; but keep moving—press ahead. Compliment yourself along the way and enjoy the dance. Someone is watching who thinks you are quite wonderful, both as a mommy and a woman.

Prayer of the Day

Dear Father above,
    Help me today to be fair with myself. Help me to remember that I am in preparation. You have a purpose and a great plan for my life. Help me to stay in Your Word, Father, for that is the place where I will receive guidance and

encouragement. I will get a compliment from You every time I open the Book. I'm stepping out in my faith by giving up a big salary and a good job. I don't want to fear the future, but at times I do. Help me to believe. Give me a teachable heart and spirit. I know You are going to use these years to teach me valuable lessons, one at a time. Clearly, You are doing a deep work in me. Help me to be still enough to hear Your voice, so I can learn from You. I want to trust and be patient. Help me to no longer desire man's praise or shallow compliments, but to desire Your approval and wisdom. My Father, I need to remember that I am a child of God. I will put my little hand in Your big one.

Early Childhood Tip

This is one of the easiest tips in the book, and also one of the most effective. I had a wonderful professor in college named Dr. David Bird. He was my instructor for most of my Early Childhood classes. One cannot complete his courses without having an intense desire to teach young children. He taught me to compliment children when you catch them doing what you wish. I used this technique in my classroom and then, of course, later, with my own little rugrats. For example, you obviously want your children to learn to listen and respect you. Comments like, "Brielle, I really like the way you put those blocks back into the container"; or "Brandy, I like the way you closed the door when you came inside. That really helps me keep the house cooler in the summer"; or "Hunter, I liked the way you didn't whine when I told you it was bedtime." Children want to please you, and they like to be complimented. Everyone likes to be complimented—whether they are age 2 or 92. Compliment your children instead of nagging. Confirm positive behavior. I guess our role now, as mothers, is to give the compliments, not receive them. Imagine that—another change!

Chapter 3

Resting in God's Hands

3

Hands

NOTHING is spared. Even my hands have changed since I've become a mother. Hands that used to write long, revealing letters to high school and college friends now write long grocery and "to do" lists to myself. Hands that at one time rubbed lotions onto my skin and my husband's tired back now rub diaper-rash ointment onto adorable little derrieres. It may be a bit foggy, but I even have a distant memory of one of my hands on top of my teammates' hands right before those big high school games. I was part of a tangled web of arms and hands—a symbol of strength and invincibility—our happy voices screaming our high school's name. Now my hands are in another type of tangled mess as I struggle to hold onto three children's hands, a diaper bag, and a purse—while attempting to get across the parking lot in one piece!

When you think about it, we identify our strength and abilities with being able to use our arms and especially our hands, don't we? A tough, cocky criminal is finally defeated and helpless when the police yank both of his hands behind his back and place handcuffs on them. A strong college athlete, his arm in a cast, sits dejected and disappointed on the bench, helplessly watching his teammates lose the championship. Your heart breaks, and you become keenly aware of the value of your hands, when you hear of people who have survived serious accidents yet become paralyzed. Left without the use of their arms and hands, they often suffer serious depression and feel their life is over. Hands and strength are tied together.

I have come upon a number of Scripture passages that speak of God's strength being shown through His hands.

Psalm 89:13
Your arm is endued with power;
   your HAND is strong, your right HAND exalted.

1 Chronicles 29:12
Wealth and honor come from you;
   you are the ruler of all things.
In your HANDS are strength and power
   to exalt and give strength to all.

Habakkuk 3:4
His splendor was like the sunrise;
   rays flashed from his HAND,
   where his power was hidden."

    Each hand that God created for us has 26 bones and 30 muscles and is the most flexible part of our bodies. It's amazing that we can do fine, delicate work with our hands, like removing a tiny splinter from our toddler's finger. Yet our hands can also move very heavy objects like beds . . . when it is bedtime and we have to find "Mr. Bear" who has fallen in between the wall and the bed. Because I've experienced all the things that my own hands can do, why then shouldn't I believe that God's hands can be intricate enough to care for me and see me through my everyday trials even while being strong enough to care for all of His creation?

    Every single person that the Almighty has created is special. You are very special to Him. Remember, your hands and mine may look similar, but let us turn them over. No two fingerprints are alike. Modern society has used fingerprinting as an effective tool to catch criminals. I'm thinkin' we should be using the truth about fingerprints to catch men and women for Christ. Absolutely! How can anyone think about the variety of fingerprints and not believe in a God that desires a personal relationship with each one of His unique children? He went to a lot of trouble to make all our hands different, each finger distinct.

Isaiah 49:2
. . . in the shadow of his HAND he hid me.

Isaiah 41:10
So do not fear, for I am with you;
  do not be dismayed, for I am your God.
I will strengthen you and help you;
  I will uphold you with my righteous right HAND.

A boldness and confidence bubbles up inside of me when I meditate on verses like these. Our hands are no longer tied behind our backs. We are free! We do not have to be prisoners to sin. Jesus stretched out His hands and took care of that for us. Our hands are free now to do God's work and God's will.

The power in our hands sometimes can't even be measured. A simple caress can change the course of a relationship. Hands that teach a deaf person's hands to do sign language give him a path out of his silent world. Wounds can start to heal when a humble father reaches out a hand to a teenage son.

Do you remember that I said our hands were the most flexible part of our body? Maybe that flexibility wasn't placed there just so we could flex them to play lovely music on the piano or guitar and receive applause. And quite possibly God had more in mind than just gifting us with finger muscles that could fly across the keyboard as we surf the internet or crunch numbers on a calculator. Perhaps our hands are ahhh, ummmmm, well . . . flexible enough so we can grasp and turn the door handle—opening the door gently this time—and apologize for slamming it earlier in anger. *Flexible* wrists. *Humble* wrists. Yep, maybe, just maybe, God created that flexibility so we might wrap our fingers around a pen and jot a note telling an estranged loved one that we were wrong and are truly sorry. *Flexible* fingers. *Humble* fingers. If we are truly followers of Christ, we must get serious about allowing our hands to become God's instruments. And I don't think we can even grasp the quiet strength that is found in our folded hands during prayer. Flexible, humble hands are strong hands!

The scriptures I've shared tell us where we must be—in *God's* hands. I imagine that sometimes, in our waywardness, impatience and rebellion, we start to wiggle through His fingers. Sometimes we want to be independent. We move. He doesn't! It's our choice—a *wrong* choice. But, we can be confident that our loving Father will never drop us. He places His other hand underneath to catch us, scoops us up and puts us back in the middle of His solid palm. You'll always know when you are in the center of *His* mighty hand. You see, there is a scar there—where a nail once was. When that scar is ever present in your mind and heart, that is when you'll discover you're in His almighty hand. You see, our Jesus has hands that changed the world!

> John 10:28
> *I give them eternal life, and they shall never perish;
> no one can snatch them out of my HAND.*

Prayer of the Day

Dear Heavenly Father,

I'm in awe of the way You made our bodies. Our hands are so strong, yet so sensitive. They help me work. They help me love. Thank You for my hands. My hands have been blessed today. I wiped away my child's little tears and I taught a little pair of hands how to tie. I smiled when I saw my children fold their precious hands in prayer while talking to you tonight, Lord. What a privilege it is to be a mother. I'm just so glad that I don't have to figure this whole "life" thing out; I can just rest in Your omnipotent hand. Amen.

Early Childhood Tip

Today's activity is a craft idea. Your kids can participate in this, but the final product is actually something for you! Where do you spend most of your waking hours? No, not the laundry room—the other place where you spend so many waking hours. Right! The kitchen. Well, since you're spending so much time there, you should at least look stylish while you are working so hard!

I hope you'll try making this handprint apron. It is cute, handmade, and functional. This craft is inexpensive too.

Everything I suggest is geared towards not breaking your budget. This author has lived on one salary for a very long time. You'll need to gather the following supplies:

- a solid-colored apron
- a few paper plates (large)
- fabric paint—make sure you have a different color for each of your kids
- fabric pen or tubes of paint to write on fabric
- a variety of decorative buttons and/or decorative small patches/decals (found in the notion section)

The day before you plan to do this activity with the kids is when you are going to do your part. On the top section of the apron, write (with a fabric pen) the words "Leave it in God's hands." Promise me that you won't be compulsive and measure where every letter should be so that it'll be evenly spaced. Just have fun and do it! I swear, no art teacher is going to show up at your door and grade you on this. Just pretend that you are back in elementary school and just enjoy playing with paints and being creative. Everyone used to be an artist. It wasn't until we got older and started judging ourselves and comparing ourselves with others that we became unartistic. Okay, that is another chapter. . . . I'll get back on track. Lay the apron flat and let it dry for 24 hours.

Next comes the messy part. This involves the kids, so prepare. Cover your workspace with an old plastic tablecloth or newspapers. Put smocks or old shirts on the kids. Put their names in a hat and draw names to pick the order for the handprinting process. Work with one child at a time. Write down which kid has which color, so you'll be able to remember when putting their names next to their prints. Now, pour some paint onto the paper plate of the child with whom you are currently working. The kids who are waiting can decorate the bottom of their plate with crayons or you may invite them to trace around their hands on a piece of paper and cut them out. This is a great hand-eye coordination activity and it will keep them busy until you can work with them.

The child simply presses his entire hand down into the paint in the paper plate, making sure the entire surface, palm and fingers, is covered with the paint. Ask him to point to the spot on the apron where he wants to place his print. Lay the apron right side up and close to him. Next, he presses his painted hand firmly onto the apron. You should press his hand down too with your own, to insure a good print. Gently grab his wrist and pull his hand straight up and off the apron. Try to avoid putting a handprint on the writing that you've already done.

Each child should do both a right and a left handprint in his color. If you have only one child, simply let him decorate the apron with lots of handprints. If you are really wacky, put your cat's or dog's pawprint on there too. The kids will love that! Try to encourage the kids to place the handprints randomly throughout the material. Remember, relax—it'll look authentic if it has a few smears and dribbles! Tell them how excited you are about having an apron that has their special handprints on it. Explain that you'll keep it forever, and that it will be a precious memento. Their hands will grow and get bigger, but you'll always have this apron to remind you of when they were little. After the handprints dry, write names under their prints. Write their names in big letters. They'll be so proud to see their name on your apron!

Now, for the finishing touches! Adorable patches and buttons are really "in" right now. You can find patches depicting little flowers, fruits, shapes and much more. There are buttons with dogs on them, smiley faces, and everything imaginable.

Grab a needle and some thread (the same color as your apron) and apply a few patches and/or attractive buttons to the neckline and pocket area of the new apron. If your apron doesn't have a pocket, you might want to add a decorative touch to the bottom of your apron. A wide ribbon or lace could also be attached to the bottom. In fact, this will probably be cheaper than the patches and buttons, yet still will create a great look. Don't forget to look at the sale table first!

When you wear your apron, I hope that you'll remember this chapter. I hope good thoughts will flood your mind that you have a loving Father in heaven who loves nothing more than to hold you in the palm of His hand. The cute little hands splashed across your apron should remind you of all the blessings you have. Children are blessings from God's hands to ours.

Chapter 4

The 4th Commandment

4

Don't Forget the Sabbath

WHAT would you say if I told you there is a tonic which you can take that will make you feel all of the things listed below?
- peaceful
  - rested
    - rejuvenated
      - calmer
        - give you a clearer vision of your life
        - give your priorities focus
      - give you wisdom
    - give you joy
  - give you a thankful heart

Would you want some of this tonic? Would it seem like an answer to prayer? Are you reaching for the phone right now, hoping I'll give you the 800 number so you can call and have the potion Fed Ex'd A.S.A.P.? We all want those things, but in our busy lives they somehow seem to elude us. We all need rest and renewal. We are running ourselves into the ground. We are on the phone, we're reading our e-mail, we're sending a fax, we're driving the soccer team to a game, we're nursing a baby, we're chasing a baby, we're watching one of the 250 channels on TV, we're cleaning our homes, we're paying the bills, we're working two jobs, we're shopping at the mall or shopping on line, we're going, going, going! Thousands of tasks and responsibilities stare us in the face and we feel like we'll never catch up.

It took me a long time to realize that I never *will* catch up! There will always be endless tasks to do. All week long, mothers care for their families. On Sunday we must stop and remember that someone takes care of us—our heavenly Father. I was forgetting to keep the Sabbath day holy. The things I promised in my tonic above can be found when you begin to really believe in and implement the 4th commandment.

Our culture tells us to work hard. People who work 24/7 are admired. But listen, our culture didn't create us, God did. He knows we're dust and very fragile beings. He put us together and knows that we require rest. I really had a breakthrough in my spiritual walk when I began to see that the Ten Commandments were not some unattainable old rules to make me miserable and oppressed, but instead, they were guidelines for me from a loving Father who was trying to deliver me from pain, heartache and death.

God tried to save us from divorce, destroyed children, and broken hearts with Number 7—"You shall not commit adultery." He tried to save us from envy, jealousy, and overworking to "keep up with the Joneses" with Number 10—"You shall not covet." And God is trying to keep us from stress, burnout, and hopelessness with Number 4— "Remember the Sabbath day by keeping it holy." The Sabbath day should be our day of refuge. A day where we are absolutely purposeless. What? *Do nothing?* I know that sounds so radical, doesn't it?

Listen, I would think it was absolutely ludicrous if my three kids came home from school and immediately went to work organizing their toys. Imagine if the following happened: First they washed their toys. On their special toys they sprayed a solvent to add shine and polish. Next they hurried to alphabetize them. Stacking and counting them followed. They rushed to and fro with little clipboards, taking notes about their toys, jotting down notes about any problems. They reorganized their toys and skipped my wonderful dinner to apply labels to most of them—meanwhile complaining about something under their breath. Friends called to play, but they turned them down, pausing a second or two to talk about their newest and most impressive toys. Papers crumbled all around them as they furiously drew up plans to build on a new room for their toys. How would I feel? My heart would surely break as they worked and worked, not ceasing... until I made them go to sleep. Maybe I would hear them later, tossing and turning upstairs. Could they be thinking about things they had left undone? As I again closed the doors of their bedrooms, I would be overcome with heaviness as I realized that they had never once enjoyed any of their toys today. Not one!

Of course, this has never happened. My children come home, play, relax, and enjoy a snack. Children seem to find balance. But what does God see when He looks down on you and me? Does He see us (His children) constantly rushing around but forgetting to even enjoy the blessings we have? Should we—no, could we—stop on the seventh day and rest like He has planned for us to do all along?

Ever the example, Jesus shows us how to keep the Sabbath holy. Over and over in the Bible we see Him getting away by Himself. He knew He needed to be with the Father. He knew He needed to quiet His spirit so he could face the pressures of life.

Mark 6:31(TLB) says, "Then Jesus suggested, 'Let's get away from the crowds for a while and rest.'" Luke 5:16 tells us "Jesus often withdrew to lonely places and prayed." Strength is given to us from God, but we must spend time with Him to receive it. Jesus obeyed the spirit inside of Him, advising Him to retreat. We too need to listen to that still, quiet voice.

What should I do on the Sabbath? Honor and hold up the Lord. That may mean different things to different people. Many Christians begin their Sabbath by worshiping at church on Sunday morning. When I see the candles lit and hear the choir start to sing, I try my best to put my life aside and focus on God. This is difficult sometimes. Grocery lists, phone calls to return, and the lunch menu try to steal my attention, but I have faith that God has a word to teach me *if* I'll only discipline myself and listen.

The rest of the day could be spent enjoying the family and resting. Let the machine pick up your phone messages. Unplug the computer and hide the remote. Enjoy a long meal with your family. Use paper plates so everyone can go for a family walk afterwards. Crack open the photo albums. Build a fire and read. Play cards or games. Steal away on your own and read a few chapters of the Bible or a Christian book or magazine. Reflect on what you've read. Invite another family over for dinner. Tell them to bring over what they have in their fridge, combine it with yours and *enjoy*. It may be a weird meal, but the point is to get together and have fun, not stress yourself out with a dinner party. Martha Stewart just had a heart attack!

You could do something crazy—like sit outside under the stars and notice the awesome light-show from our Lord. Go to the park and commune with nature. Try to avoid doing tasks that will cause you to worry. Pay the bills and make your "to do" lists on Friday or Saturday, not on Sunday. End the day with devotions with your kids. There are loads of excellent children's devotional books at Christian bookstores—from toddler to teenager in range. You will be surprised at how up-to-date they are. They deal with issues that your children will relate to. Use this time to share your values with your children. Your child's Sunday school teacher is not responsible for your child's spiritual growth—you are. If you spend some time on Sunday sharing God with them, they'll realize that learning about their faith is a valuable thing.

I guess you could say our family's Sabbath begins at a local doughnut shop before church. We started doing this about four years ago. No matter how busy the weekend gets, the kids know that they have our attention on Sunday mornings. And somehow in between bites of Dutch crumb doughnuts and "everything bagels" we find some "rest." It's a time of laughing, teasing, and reflections on the week.

Can you rest and relax every Sunday? Of course not; you must be flexible. But you can probably do it two out of four Sundays if you want to. You must chase after the things that you want. Chase peace and joy. After a while you won't have to . . . you'll realize you already had them.

Ignoring the Sabbath is like choosing to ignore the delicious desserts on the dessert cart after an unsatisfying meal. How could you do that? Ignoring the Sabbath is like spending the entire day at the best amusement park and never getting on one single ride. Ridiculous! Ignoring the Sabbath is like walking through the Sahara desert and ignoring the lush oasis just yards ahead. Crazy! When we see what God wants to do for us through this day of rest, we realize how foolish we are in giving it up. For what? Do we value our spiritual lives? Are we interested in immediate physical gratification, or do we crave deep spiritual satisfaction? Do we want to stay in bed, read the paper and have brunch, or do we want to walk in victory through all the twists and turns of our week knowing that Jesus Christ is beside us and cares for us?

Satan will try to sabotage your Sabbath day. In fact, expect it! He knows that you will start changing your life and lifestyle when you become radical about resting and feeding your spirituality. Satan realizes that when we slow down and give God first place in our hearts and minds, then we become powerful, joyful, and our priorities align to bring us peace. The world we live in works to seduce us away from discovering any sort of inner balance. There are so many other fun and exciting things to do besides attending church. Plus, you know the churches are full of hypocrites anyway! Besides, it's your only day to sleep in and the sermons are so boring. We must decide whose voice we're going to listen to. The Bible warns us of this.

When we give up our Sabbath day, something will suffer. It could be our marriage, our relationships with our children, our health, or most importantly, our spiritual life. Oh, Satan is so subtle. It won't happen quickly. If it did, then we would be clever enough to identify the problem and correct it expediently. No, it happens slowly. For example, a mother feels pressure to make more money, so she decides to work Saturdays—then, eventually, on Sundays too. She never gets to church anymore, but she rationalizes her decision and says that she'll read the Bible on her lunch hour or when she gets home from work. The Bible stays untouched on her shelf, her marriage slowly dies, she sees her kids less and they stop attending Sunday school . . . and over time the mother develops many stress-like physical symptoms—all for some extra money. God would have heard her prayers of financial need if she would've humbled herself to ask. Attending church with her family, being a good example to her children, and refreshing her spirit are more valuable than any extra silver coins. God always gives us choices. But there are consequences to those choices.

I remember when I was a little girl . . . our family would go for Sunday drives! I loved to sing along with the radio while sitting in the back seat. A Sunday drive? That is unheard of today. No one just gets in the car and drives. Today, we have a plan, a mission, a list of stops to conquer! I remember when stores were closed on Sundays. My kids looked at me in astonishment when I explained that businesses formerly stayed closed due to the Sabbath. Well, those days are gone. We can only respond to the present. I don't think the cash register drawers will ever be still again. I'm afraid that shopping has become America's favorite pastime. I'm not saying that shopping is bad. We all need to buy goods. I am saying that it is sad that "shopping" is the focus for many on the Sabbath. The catalogs and ads on television convince us that if we buy their products, their clothes, their stuff, then we'll look happy and content and free like the lovely people in their ads. What a facade! Things are not making us happier. We must choose to carve out a peaceful day to nourish ourselves and those we love. Don't worry about what others are doing. Listen to the Holy Spirit inside of you. Has His voice been begging you to slow down?

God doesn't want us to get legalistic. I believe He wants us to enjoy our lives. But He desires a closeness with us. He wants to renew our spirits on the Sabbath so that we can face the challenges of our busy week. Don't you think that He wants to help you with all the responsibilities and struggles you'll encounter this week? *He does.* But if we don't give Him our time and be still under Him, how will we know in what direction we are to go?

> Psalm 25:14 (TLB)
> *Friendship with God is reserved for those who reverence him.*
> *With them alone he shares the secrets of his promises.*

He'll share His secrets with me? I need wisdom.

> Psalm 46:10
> *Be still, and know that I am God.*

Be still? I've forgotten how. Show me, Lord.

All of this is available to us if only we seek it. Setting aside time for goodness, for God, and for our spiritual well-being is valuable, even if the world says it is not.

Observing the Sabbath can be like a tonic. This tonic is not only delicious, it is also powerful and quite intoxicating! I want you to have it! And if you already have it, I want you to share it with someone who doesn't have it! Protect it. Unlike many of the world's products, this tonic delivers on all of its promises. Satisfaction is guaranteed. God will not let you down. Allow yourself a rest. Work hard for six days, and then look around you and realize "it is good" and rest on the seventh. Serendipity is enjoying a lovely purposeless afternoon and discovering the 4th commandment tonic for the body, heart and soul. Cheers!!!!!

Prayer of the Day

Father,

My mind and body know that I need to slow down and simplify, but it is difficult for me to put this into practice. I get caught up in my plans and forget about Your bigger plan. Thank You for the Sabbath. Thank You for the wisdom of resting. Help me to honor Your day. I desire to be still and hear Your voice, I do. Teach me how. Help me to fight the temptations that the world attractively displays to draw me away from You, Your church, and my spiritual life. I know that, as a mother, I set the tone in my home. May the resonances be calm melodies, joined by peaceful harmonies on the Lord's Day. I will not be a fool and skip such a beautiful song composed just for God's children. Just for me! I'm going to start listening to a different drummer! Amen.

Early Childhood Activity

For a change of pace, today's activity is a cooking project. A perfect Sunday afternoon project which will tie in nicely with our topic of "resting." I've included information and ideas for you to use as conversation starters for your older children. Your little guys will just enjoy creating, eating, and getting dough in their hair!

I picked German soft pretzels because

1) they are delicious!
2) for a snack, they are guilt free—only 3g. fat and 130 calories
3) they contain yeast which requires kneading and RESTING
4) the origin of the pretzel has Christian roots.

It is believed that 7th century monks were the first to produce pretzels. The monks offered pieces of baked dough to young children as a reward after they memorized prayers. The pretzel design represented a person in prayer. The early monks crossed their arms in front of them, resting their hands on opposite shoulders while praying. The yummy pretzels were called "pretiola," which means "little rewards." It's also been said that the pretzel shape came into being to remind us of the Trinity. The three holes (representing the Father, Son, and Holy Ghost) of the pretzel are evident, yet the pretzel braid is one continuous strand.

As you follow the recipe below, you'll be asked to knead the dough. This stretches the dough, making it resilient so it can rise and get fluffy. As you pull and stretch the dough, talk about how during your children's week they too may feel pulled and pushed around; i.e., homework assignments, disappointments with friends, dealing with classmates and teachers that may (at times) get on their nerves, parents telling them to clean their rooms or complete chores. Tell them you feel pulled during the week too.

Next, after the pushing and pulling, the dough gets to "rest." It is during this phase that the flavor development takes place. The yeast begins to feed on the sugars and begins to release bubbles. Explain how we need rest too; that that is why God, in His wisdom and care for us, made the Sabbath. He knew we would need to rest after being pulled and pushed around all week. Ahhhh! Doesn't it feel good to relax and rest? When we feed on God's Word (read the Bible) and fellowship with other Christians, we will develop flavor. We will grow, too, just like this dough is going to grow.

In step 4 of the recipe you will be adding salt to your pretzels. See Mark 9:50. We are to be salt in this world. Salt adds flavor. We are to add flavor to the world for the Lord. God says we are to be like salt. Salt preserves things. Explain that long ago people would put salt on their meat to preserve it, because they did not have refrigerators. The meat would last and last. We must preserve our Sabbath day. If your children know it is important to you, it'll become important to them. Train up a child in the way that he should go . . . .

Now, go . . . go get the mustard and your aprons and get cookin'!

• German Soft Pretzels •

These soft, yeasty pretzels are best served warm from the oven. Excellent with mustard on the side. You'll need:

> 1 package active dry yeast
> 1 cup warm water (about 110° F.)
> 2 tablespoons vegetable oil
> 1 tablespoon sugar
> 1/3 cup baking soda
> 2 1/2 to 3 cups of all-purpose flour
> 6 cups of water
> coarse (kosher) salt
> mustard (optional)

1) Sprinkle yeast over warm water in a medium-sized bowl; let stand until foamy (about 5 minutes). Add sugar, oil, and 1 1/2 cups of the flour; beat until smooth. Gradually stir in 1 cup more flour.

2) Turn dough out onto a floured cutting board and knead until smooth and satiny (about 5 minutes), adding more flour as needed to prevent sticking. Melt 2 tablespoons of butter in the microwave and pour into a large mixing bowl. Place the kneaded dough into the bowl; turn over to grease top. Cover the bowl with plastic wrap and let rise in a warm place until doubled (about 1 hour). Make sure it is covered; the dough likes a draft-free environment along with warmth. I usually cover the bowl with plastic wrap, then put a kitchen towel over it and place the covered bowl in a sunny spot in the kitchen.

3) Next, punch dough down and knead briefly on a lightly floured board to release air. Cut dough into 12 equal pieces. Working with one piece at a time (keep remaining dough covered), roll (with your hands) into a smooth rope about 18 inches long and twist into a pretzel shape. Arrange slightly apart on greased baking sheets, placing loose ends underneath. Let rise, uncovered, in a warm place until puffy (about 25 minutes).

4) Bring the six cups of water and the baking soda to a boil in a 3-quart stainless steel or enamel pan (don't use aluminum); reduce heat to keep mixture boiling gently. With a slotted spatula, lower pretzels, one at a time, into water and simmer, turning once, for 10 seconds on each side. Lift from water and drain on a cooling rack. Let dry briefly; then sprinkle with kosher salt. Use two greased cookie sheets. Put six pretzels on each.

5) Bake in a 425° oven until golden brown (10-12 min.).

Watch carefully. Serve warm or at room temperature. To reheat, place on baking sheets and heat, uncovered, in a 400° oven until warm (about 10 min.). Serve with mustard, if desired. Makes about 8-10 delicious pretzels.

Show the children that this was a recipe that required very few ingredients. The ingredients were quite simple: yeast, salt, flour, water. Many times good things come from very simple things!

Chapter 5

Spiritual Gifts

5

Thank You for the Gift

Romans 12:6–8

We have different gifts, according to the grace given us. If a man's gift is prophesying, let him use it in proportion to his faith. If it is serving, let him serve; if it is teaching, let him teach; if it is encouraging, let him encourage; if it is contributing to the needs of others, let him give generously; if it is leadership, let him govern diligently; if it is showing mercy, let him do it cheerfully.

It's comforting to know and see that some things have not changed. I have been admitted to a hospital three times; those were when I delivered our three children. Overprotective from the get-go, I kept each baby in my hospital room most of the time, but when I needed a little snooze, I asked the nurse to take the baby to the nursery. I recall how, after a much needed nap, I awoke and felt the need to nurse my newborn and to kiss ten new little toes once again, so I walked—no, make that waddled—down the hall to the nursery. The hospital nursery had a big glass window and rows and rows of tiny bassinets, as it has for decades. Some proud parents, grandparents and other family members were pointing, beaming, and discussing which family traits their new baby possessed, while peering through the glass. What a lovely gathering!

I hope the glassed-in nursery will always stay the same. I'm scared that in the future someone might propose drywalling over the glass and setting up computer monitors that will feed pictures to working family member's computers. How sad it would be for people to miss out on jokes about the baby having Uncle Richard's double chin or jibes about how the baby drools just like Grandpa. What a happy place this is, this space outside a simple glass wall.

After the boisterous crowd walked down the hallway that day with arms filled with gifts, bouquets and balloons, I made my way to the glass nursery window for my turn, and found my little baby in her glass bassinet. She looked so warm and content in her pink blanket and pink-and-white knit hat. The bassinet was small, yet she was so tiny that she looked like a pink peanut inside of it. I looked at all the other babies in the nursery. From my vantage point, they all looked fairly similar except, of course, the girls were wrapped in pink blankets and the boys in blue.

I couldn't actually see this, but in my mind's eye I imagined each baby's talents wrapped up in lovely wrapping paper and placed inside their bassinets with them. Talents . . . just waiting to be discovered and "unwrapped" in each child's future, making each child special and unique. The babies lying in this nursery may have looked the same then, but just wait. Each baby—every baby—is born with natural talents. God gave them those special natural skills and abilities.

Some gifts are so obvious, are they not? For example, if you don't use a box when gift-wrapping a football it's pretty obvious to the recipient of the present that it *is* a football. That is the way some of our talents come. They are just obvious. Some babies grow up to be excellent artists, musicians, architects, athletes or actors. In such cases, the talent is obvious. God used the "no-box present" approach with such people.

Now, as for some of the others, I imagined that their talents were somewhat concealed in those trendy new gift bags—those with the fancy confetti or shaved paper tucked in around the gifts. Most of us had gift-bag talents in our bassinets. For us, people could see only the top of the gift. We knew we had a little talent, but we had to "grow into it." Our talent was there, just not so obvious.

And yet there are other kinds of gifts. These are the spiritual gifts. Imagine these each being like a gift that is wrapped in a big box with the most elegant of paper. The top has a gold and silver cascading bow on it. These gifts are given to us from our heavenly Father, but we do not receive them at birth. They are not to be found in our bassinets. When we make a decision to give our hearts to Jesus, it is then that we receive these gifts.

A spiritual gift is a supernatural ability given to us the minute we are saved—bestowed without cost. It is given to us to glorify God by encouraging others in the Church—the worldwide body of Christ—and to spread the "good news" of God's Kingdom. A talent enriches your life. A gift enriches the Church and honors our Father in heaven. Paul urges us to "eagerly desire the greater gifts" (1 Corinthians 12:31).

Some of the spiritual gifts are: leading, teaching, wisdom, mercy, hospitality, administration, discernment of spirits, faith, giving, helping, exhortation, knowledge, shepherding, evangelism, and prophecy.

A Christian woman who opens her home continually to others, feeds the youth group, holds Bible studies, and plans social functions tirelessly at the church is blessed with the gift of hospitality. Planning a food drive at Thanksgiving for the homeless, and sewing baby blankets for orphans in Russia are activities done by women demonstrating their gifts of mercy. Your pastor nurtures the flock and unwraps his or her gift of shepherding. It is important to remember that the woman using her "quiet" gift of helping by changing diapers and feeding babies in the cribbery is just as important as the pastor, even though his/her gift may be more noticeable. God sees into our hearts. God will honor us when we use our gifts. The gifts may be different, but they have the same goal. We are to unwrap our gifts, and to enjoy others' gifts, while not coveting theirs or comparing ours with theirs. Isn't it just like our Jesus to go above and beyond? Not only did Jesus give us the gift of salvation, He also gives us gifts He knows we can use to uphold His Church by working together with fellow Christians as lights in a dark world.

My favorite presents are the ones in big boxes. You open the box and find a big present inside, happily unwrap it, and then the giver enthusiastically tells you to keep digging because there are more presents at the bottom! I love that! You blush and tell them that they shouldn't have. Each little gift is unwrapped and is even better than the one preceding it. You feel like you are five years old, and you never want the surprises to end. You marvel at how your friend knew exactly what you needed and wanted! What a friend!

That is the way your spiritual gift is. You pray and ask God to help you to recognize your gift. You find your gift and open it; then you start using it in your local church and its outreaches in the neighborhood and beyond. It is easy, gives you such fulfillment, and fits you like a glove. The work and serving brings you joy. But wait, God has other gifts for you in this box. You dig down into the box and discover lots of little packages. Oh, how our Father must enjoy seeing us open the little packages—the little blessings He plants inside to follow our gift. Blessings and more blessings! How does He know exactly what you need and what you desire? What a friend! What a relationship! Each gift is handmade. It was made for you! He could hardly wait to give it to you. He blessed you with your *talents* back when you arrived and slept peacefully in your little bassinet. But He held onto this *gift* for last. It was placed inside of you that special day when you asked Him to be your Savior.

Some people haven't opened their spiritual gift yet. They've been "saved" or "born again" for quite some time, yet the gift sits on the shelf unopened. It is still wrapped up tightly; no one has even shaken it and tried to guess its contents. How sad for these people when they get to heaven and God asks them, "What did you do with the spiritual gift I lovingly gave you?" Perhaps they'll say, "I just didn't have time to open that gift, but I faithfully sat in church on Sunday"; "I was busy making money using my many talents"; "I don't think You gave me a gift; I never saw it"; "I was planning on doing some things in the church when I had some free time." I truly believe that the reason why so many people feel empty is that they are achieving satisfaction on one level—using their talents and making money—but because they do not use their spiritual gift they continue to feel incomplete. Could that incompleteness be a warning?

We live in an upside-down world. Volunteering, teaching Sunday school, leading a youth group, being a mentor, becoming a missionary, going to a Women's Bible Study, or foregoing a career to stay home and raise your children all seem like a waste of time to some people. We're successful if we have climbed the corporate ladder, own our own business, have a full-time career or compile an impressive stock portfolio. *Let us defy* the materialism and greed of our contemporary culture! God has promised to never leave us or forsake us. That means *never*! The decisions we make about our children, families, and our time have eternal value and consequences. Hang on! Jump right in; rip off the lovely paper; let the ribbons tumble around you; let the tape break as you open your gift and discover what God has chosen to give you!!!!

Other scripture concerning spiritual gifts:
1 Corinthians 12:27–31, 1 Peter 4:9–11.

Prayer of the Day

Heavenly Father,
Have I thanked You for my talents lately? Thank You for the things that I can do so easily and effortlessly. I sometimes dwell on the things I cannot do. Today, help me to thank You over and over for the talents You've blessed me with.

And thank You for my spiritual gifts. I feel Your gentle hand guiding me as I discover and develop them. I understand and accept that You will test my character and promote me to even more responsibilities in due season. Keep me humble in knowing and understanding the price paid for this gift of mine—Christ's precious blood at the base of a rugged cross. May the hands serving and giving be mine, but may the glory always return to You.

When I get discouraged and tired, help me to draw my strength from Your promises. When I don't see immediate results from the things that I do at church, help me not to give up but to keep going. Satan will try to convince me that I have no talents and gifts, or lie to me about not being "good enough" to serve a holy God. I know better. My gift from You is awesome and it is just filled with lots of little blessings that I'm not about to miss. Guide me always. Amen.

Early Childhood Tip

All of us busy moms spend a small fortune on buying birthday gifts for our children's friends. How can we send our kids to a birthday party with a nice gift but still keep a little cash in our purse? Try these hints. Keep your eyes (ads) and ears (radio spots) open for sales at the large-chain toy stores. In my area, the big sales are usually at the end of the summer. Shop during the big sale where you can save 30-60% on toys, books and videos. One summer I spent around $120, which seemed ridiculous at the time. However, I purchased over 15 gifts, and I did all the shopping in one hour for that school year's birthday parties! That beats going out to the store on 15 separate occasions and wasting time looking and waiting in line.

Next, purchase giftwrap when you see it on sale. Keep the giftwrap with the gifts and ribbon. Instead of buying expensive bows—which look pretty, but which the little kids toss—I buy a large spool of ribbon and a huge bag of Blow Pops (lollipops). Kids of all ages love them, and they look so cute and inviting on top of any present. Put three lollipops together and tie them securely with masking tape. Then tie colorful ribbon around the lollipops. Make sure some of the ribbon dangles, and use the sides of your scissors to make the bottom of the ribbon curly. Secure the lollipops to the top of your gift. Believe me, I've never seen one little kid toss them! Keep your large bag of lollipops with your giftwrap, gifts and ribbon. That way you'll be able to find everything quickly.

I rarely buy cards for my children's friends. Birthday cards cost about $2.50 to $4.00 a card. My children enjoy making cards for their friends. At one time, they would just have used heavy white paper, crayons and markers, but today they are enjoying creating professional-looking cards on the computer. A program that our family has enjoyed is called "The Print Shop Publishing Suite" by Broderbund. You can write to them at 500 Redwood Blvd., Novato, CA 94948-6121, or reach them on the Web at www.broderbund.com. If you don't have a computer, try spicing-up your card-making sessions with a package of cool stickers, stamps, and gold and silver stamp pads; or try some of the new pens that write in glitter, or in wild neon colors that show up well on black paper! Be creative. When you care enough to send the very best you should make it yourself!

Chapter 6

Accepting Our Children

6

Ones, Twos and Threes

"WHERE should your hands be, Hunter?" I asked. I waited patiently to see if my six-year-old would remember my cue. Quickly, my son, Hunter, pulled his tiny hands onto his lap and tried to concentrate on the worksheet in front of him. I looked at this slight, blond little person beside me and wrestled with the questions in my mind. Why is he struggling so much in his kindergarten class? Should I keep him in this private school or look for an easier, less-stressful environment. Originally, I had felt so good about my decision to send him to a Christian preschool, but now I was wondering if I should have sent him to a more academically-oriented program so he could compete with all the bright students sitting in his school classroom. I know I'm not alone. Many mothers have children that struggle academically.

I tutor Hunter a few times during the week. His teacher mentioned that following directions was a weak area for my son. I told Hunter that at school, and at home, he should put his hands in his lap while the directions are being given. This way his hands won't be tempted to touch crayons and pencils. I was proud of him for remembering this new "cue," and for trying so hard.

While Hunter practiced a paper on making the numerals 2 and 3, I stared out the window at our yard covered with a blanket of February snow. I glanced down at his work and noticed that he was reversing the numbers again. I felt frustration building inside me. How many times have I reviewed this with him? Too many to count. The enemy whispered in my ear: "Think of all the time you could have to do other things if you didn't have to spend this time doing schoolwork with Hunter. Other kids are probably going to tease him. He could have major problems. How is that going to look?—you are a teacher." I could feel the self-pity settling over me—thick and heavy. Satan delights in that, doesn't he?

I looked at my son. He smiled up at me and did his best on the worksheet in front of him. Why do we let ourselves worry about so many things? I know that God put Hunter together exactly the way Hunter needs to be to serve God in the future. Hunter was born with just the perfect mix of strengths and weaknesses. God will shape and mold this little boy. Why can't I have more faith? I only need to accept him the way he is. *Accept. Have patience. Trust.* Uggghhhh . . . .

"Hunter, why don't we stop for today," I said sweetly. I don't want him to become frustrated when we "do school." "Good job, hon," I said.

He was thrilled to be finished. He threw his arms around me for a quick hug and went out the door. "I bet he is on his way to play Nintendo," I sighed, and felt the hot tears rolling down my cheeks. "I wish it wasn't so hard for him." It is very difficult for us to watch our children struggle. Does our heavenly Father wince in pain when we struggle to follow Him and keep failing—tripping ourselves up?

I wiped the tears from my face and ran my fingers through my curly hair. It was then that I spied them: I hate them; they are everywhere in my house. Laundry baskets. Laundry baskets filled with clean clothes that need to be put away. I moaned and decided to keep moving on my list of "Mommy Things To Do Today." If I was going to feel sorry for myself, I could at least be productive while doing it.

As I was pondering the phenomenon of why my three children tell me they have nothing to wear and how it is that I can't seem to stuff any of these clean clothes into their drawers (due to the fact that they are already filled with other clean clothes), I noticed a little voice behind me. "I made a picture for you, Mama," Hunter exclaimed with a warm smile. His big brown eyes sparkled. He wasn't playing Nintendo after all. Wow! "Tell me about it?" I asked, as I plopped down on his bed. Hunter crawled into my lap and unfolded the paper in his tiny fist. "It is Jesus on the cross. I made Jesus green, my favorite color. Do you see His smile?" he said, proudly. "Honey,

I love this picture and I know Jesus does too. Why did you make Jesus with that big smile?" I asked, while I reached into the laundry basket for a clean shirt. "Jesus is smiling because He loves me soooooo much," Hunter said confidently. I stopped and literally froze. God spoke to me so clearly—right in my ear. I understood. God whispered . . . Yes, Hunter struggles making those 2's and 3's, but Liz, Hunter KNOWS ME! This little child already knows and understands the essence of ME—many adults don't even have that!!! God helped me to see my son, not as a struggler, but a leader. Gifted in all the right things. He knows and loves the Lord. I giggled a little, and this time wiped away the happy tears that were sliding down my cheeks. I have to laugh sometimes when God grabs me and shoves the big lenses in front of my eyes.

Scripture for Today

Psalm 139:13–16

For you created my inmost being; you knit me together in my mother's womb. I praise you because I am fearfully and wonderfully made; your works are wonderful, I know that full well. My frame was not hidden from you when I was made in the secret place. When I was woven together in the depths of the earth, your eyes saw my unformed body. All the days ordained for me were written in your book before one of them came to be.

Jeremiah 1:4–5

The word of the Lord came to me, saying, "Before I formed you in the womb I knew you, before you were born I set you apart; I appointed you a prophet to the nations."

Also look at Galatians 1:15–17.

Prayer of the Day

Jesus,
    Be with our children. Help us as parents to be patient and kind. Help us, wise Counselor, to keep things in perspective. An education is certainly important. Our children will need

to know many things to survive in this ever-changing world. Oh, but Lord, help us to remember that the main task before us as parents is to guide our children to You. We need to show them Your words, Your life, Your cross, Your empty tomb, Your LOVE. If they know these things, then everything else will fall into place. It is as easy as ones, twos and threes!

Early Childhood Tip

If your youngster struggles with visual or memory skills he or she may copy letters or numbers incorrectly. Usually this problem is developmental and will disappear by the 2nd grade. (Our vision is not totally formed until the age of seven.) When you practice letters or numbers with your child, do it on a chalkboard or whiteboard that uses an erasable marker. This way, when a mistake is made, you can point it out, erase it quickly, and he can try again. The error is gone. When you only use paper and pencil, the errors are there (making the child feel like a failure). Erasing makes the paper look sloppy. Children care.

Yet another great idea is to to take a cookie sheet and spread a layer of pudding on it. Your child can use his finger to make letters and numbers. What a yummy way to practice! If you don't have pudding in the pantry, then use shaving cream (no tasting in this case!).

Another idea is to buy some pieces of sandpaper at Home Depot or any hardware store. Trace, then cut out large letters, both upper and lower case. Encourage your child to trace the sandpaper letters with his fingers. Ask him to close his eyes and trace with his fingers. This is a way of encouraging tactile/kinesthetic memory.

Chapter 7

Christian Literature

7

Becoming a Kingdom Bookworm

MY HUSBAND wants to retire near the water. Me, I don't care where we spend our silver years. The only thing I care about is that the place must have a library nearby. I'm quite confident that my retirement years, just like my early childhood years, will have books as an integral part of them. I love books—always have. As a little girl, I would look forward to Saturday when my mother would drop me off at the library while she went to the grocery store. This was in the 1960s and I lived in a small town, so don't gasp. I remember the librarians knowing me by name. I thought they looked so smart in their dresses, heels and pearls. I felt so powerful when they would allow me to slip behind the counter (on slow days) and stamp my own cards with the return date! And I'm grateful for growing up at a time when the library's children's section looked like a set from the play "Oliver." There were no distractions—no computer games, no CD section, no puppets, games, or arts and crafts like you find in today's library. There were aisles of books and a wooden bench with a teepee-style slanted top. The law of the land was "absolute silence." I repeat, I'm grateful that it was just me and the books.

Just as God inspired men centuries ago to write the books and letters that would later become the Bible, He still prompts men and women to write excellent Christian literature today. Have you taken advantage of these books yet? Nothing could or should take the place of the Bible. It stands alone. However, contemporary Christian books certainly supplement the Bible by giving us background information and practical applications for our daily lives.

When you attend a play or show in a well-constructed theater, you should be able to see the stage no matter where your seat is located. Your eyes and attention will be directed to the platform. Each seat in the theater must be constructed to enable viewers to see the stage, or what is the point? The architect who designed the theater is clearly in the wrong field if even one seat points away from the stage, leaving the occupant to stare in another direction. Likewise, a deserving Christian book should point you to Christ. He and His Word should be center stage. If the author is successful, the reader will begin the book by standing in the doorway of the theater, peering in to catch a glimpse of what is on stage, and finish the book in the front rows (the best seats in the house), not being able to take his eyes off of the stage—maybe even asking for an encore!

Maturing in my Christian walk began when I started taking advantage of today's Christian books. Yes, the secular bestsellers would entertain me, but not change me. I wanted to spend my time reading something that would help me understand my spiritual journey, illuminate my stumbling blocks, and help me progress in my relationship with Jesus.

I started reading Christian paperbacks while breastfeeding my children. I did not have a clue as to how much time I would be sitting and nursing during the day. Most of the time I loved nursing my children: the closeness, the bonding. But some days, because it required so much patience, it was difficult to enjoy. On bad days I viewed myself as Daisy the Cow, and wondered if the day would ever come when I would have my blouse on more than off! Good news—this is an excellent time to start reading! When the baby wants to nurse, grab a book and try not to look at it as wasted time, but a chance to recharge your battery with a book that helps you grow in your heart and spirit.

I think you'll be surprised at the wide array of subjects crowding the shelves of your local Christian bookstore. Once you tap into this heaven-sent resource, you'll have trouble walking out of the store without a hot credit card! And don't forget about your church's library. Use *it* also.

There are some definite myths about these shops. For example: *Myth*—Christian bookstores sell only Bibles and helpful curriculum for sweet, little old Sunday school teachers. *Truth*—Whoa! Are you in for a big surprise! Yes, of course, you'll find books targeting Sunday school teachers, but you'll find so much more. There are inspiring daily devotional books for everyone in the family, books about heaven, advice for teenagers, for handling trials, about weight loss, hope, angels, and much more! As you walk toward the checkout counter, you'll probably fill your arms with a new Christian pop CD for yourself, a CD-ROM with Bible stories for the kids, an inspirational mug for your hubby, a box of cute and funny greeting cards, and a Christian video for the family to watch! By the time I unload my arms at the checkout counter, I'm also sporting a cappuccino mustache and my blouse is sprinkled with cookie crumbs—from my visit to the store's coffee bar.

I am blessed to live near a large city. I can take advantage of a variety of Christian bookstores. I hope that your town has a Christian bookstore and that I've inspired you to stop in and check it out. Many books are in paperback and are quite affordable. However, if you don't have a bookstore near you, you can log onto either www.clcusa.org or www.christianbook.com. These are all-Christian websites. You'll be able to order books and have them delivered right to your door.

To get you started, I'm going to recommend some books and authors. I am thankful to God that when He urged these men and women to write, they chained themselves to their typewriters and obeyed. Talent and anointing are obvious when one opens the books penned by these devoted Christians.

>   Max Lucado -
>   *In the Eye of the Storm*
>   *He Still Moves Stones*
>   *A Gentle Thunder* (or anything ever written by this wonderful author)
> John Pollock - *A Life of Jesus*
> David Jeremiah - *Escape the Coming Night*
> Joseph F. Girzone - *Joshua*
> Joyce Meyer - *Battlefield of the Mind*
> Billy Graham - *Hope for the Troubled Heart*
> Jessie Penn-Lewis - *Thy Hidden Ones*

Look, a big, fat Butterball turkey is the main event on your Thanksgiving table. Even so, complementing it with creamy mashed potatoes, moist dressing, and sweet pumpkin pie seems both logical and necessary, and helps you enjoy the flavor of the turkey. Yes, the Bible may be all we need. When we pray for wisdom and discernment and have personal Bible study, God begins to reveal the Word to us. But isn't it wonderful that growing Christians can complement their Bible study with satisfying side dishes of contemporary Christian literature?

Scripture for Today

Proverbs 4:5–8
Get wisdom, get understanding; do not forget my words or swerve from them. Do not forsake wisdom, and she will protect you; love her, and she will watch over you. Wisdom is supreme; therefore get wisdom. Though it cost all you have, get understanding. Esteem her, and she will exalt you; embrace her, and she will honor you.

Hebrews 6:1
Therefore let us leave the elementary teachings about Christ and go on to maturity, not laying again the foundation of repentance from acts that lead to death, and of faith in God. . . .

Prayer of the Day

Heavenly Father,

Thank You for my black leatherbound book with the pretty, gold-trimmed pages. Inside is a map and guide for me in this crazy world. I want to get to know You better. So please lead me to good books that have a message that my heart needs to hear. Let me be humble enough to know that I still have so much to learn. I know that if I'm not growing, expanding my mind and reaching for a deeper relationship with You, then I'm stagnating. But, O Lord, I want your Bible to be more than just words. I don't want to be the kind of deadened Christian that merely *reads* about love, kindness and mercy. I know the words need to pierce my sin-prone soul, and my heart and mouth need to show forth love, kindness and mercy. Help me. Be patient with me as I learn to navigate this narrow path. Guide me. Don't leave me alone.

I'm going to read something positive today. Something uplifting! May I gain understanding and wisdom from those who are Your faithful servants and have written about You and Your Word. I know that You speak through others. Of all the books I've ever read or ever will read, may your "Good Book" always have first place in my heart, now and forever. Amen.

Early Childhood Tip

Every wise parent understands the importance of reading books to his or her child. Today I would like to share with you some easy ways to enrich and invigorate your "book time" with your child. As an elementary school teacher and private reading tutor for many years, I incorporated these tips into my reading lessons; and as a stay-at-home mother I have used them regularly during "book time" with my own brood.

When your child starts formal reading instruction in school, the reading teacher will be asking your child to sift through a story and find things like the main characters, the setting, the sequence of events, the main idea, the problem and solution, the title, and much more. If you start helping your child identify these things at an early age, it will help him significantly in both his reading and writing later on. (While Johnny is young and at home with you, you can be very sneaky about it. He won't even know that you are actually teaching him reading skills.)

Reading time with Mom and/or Dad should first of all be a pleasurable activity, so do not question your children after every book that you read to them. But once a week (I suggest that you pick a particular day of the week so you don't forget), tell Johnny and Mary before you read the story that you are going to be asking them some questions afterwards. You could say, "You'll need to pay close attention because I'm going to be asking you to be a detective today."

Once the book is read, you could ask a few of these questions. (Start with just a few. Do not overwhelm.) You might ask, "Who were the people or characters in the story? Who was the main character—the story was mainly about whom?" Don't be afraid to use big vocabulary words with them, but follow them up by putting it in simpler terms. Then ask, "What was the title of the story?" Help them realize that the title has to do with what happened in the story, or sometimes the characters. Now, play this silly exercise with them (my kids loved this because it was so ridiculous). Tell them that you have a better idea for the title than what is on the front of the book, and then make up a crazy title that has nothing whatsoever to do with the story. For example, let's say you just read the children's classic *The Three Little Bears* to your little ones. Declare to your tots that you think a better title would have been *Eating Spaghetti on the Way to the Moon*. They'll laugh while you continue to act shocked that they don't think it is a marvelous title. "Well, what about . . . ?" (you'll continue with more outrageous titles). Then say a title that actually could be substituted appropriately. "Would *The Day Goldilocks Learned a Lesson* be a good title?" you might ask. "Why?" Your children will learn that titles sum up the story and/or must be about the story. Very sneaky.

More "detective" questions could be: "Where did the story take place?" If they give you the wrong answer, don't reply with a flat "No." Instead, say, "You are really thinking, but let Mommy give you some clues." When they do respond with the correct answer, repeat their answer, and say, "Yes, the forest (in *The Three Bears* story) is the SETTING!" To encourage creative thinking ask, "How did the story end?" After their reply, challenge them to come up with a different ending. Accept their answers, but continue to teach them that even their ending should pertain to the characters and/or have something to do with the existing story itself.

When I was tutoring, I saw so many children struggling with creative writing. I truly believe that if we as parents start initiating creative dialogue with our children at a very early age, like the examples I've just shared, creative writing would come much more naturally to the 3rd-grade-and-up student starting out in creative writing.

Moving along to harder, higher-level thinking, you could ask questions like: "Was there a problem in the story?" and "How did they solve it? What was the solution?" When you point out that usually a story has a problem and a solution, you are teaching them much about good storytelling which will later translate into their own engaging, creative writing—someday. Double Sneaky.

Sequencing is another important reading skill. Return to the beginning of the story and put the book in sequential order out loud. Using terms like "First this happened . . . next . . . and finally" is great because they will hear their future teachers use them later. Perhaps, once the "detective book time" is an established routine, you'll want to challenge your youngsters by scrambling up the events. They love games where you goof up. They enjoy telling us that we are wrong! For example, condense the story and tell them the sequence of events, but in the wrong order. They'll enjoy pointing out that you are totally wrong and hopefully will be able to give you the correct order of events for the story.

You are your child's first teacher. Enjoy that role! I'm going to try my very best to give you some tools in this book to harness your child's creativity and motivation, so that he or she is an "active" participant in the learning process. Books and reading will be a huge part of your child's life. Make your "book time" enjoyable. While you're being sneaky, Johnny will be learning and having fun too!

Chapter 8

Women of the Bible

8

Ruth

*T*ODAY I invite you to read the book in the Bible called Ruth. I realize, of course, it may actually take you a few days to complete it. (Even though others may assume that we stay-at-home moms have lots of time on our hands to read, I know better!) So, let your Bible move with you throughout the day. So what if it gets some water spots on the pages from wild toddler-waves at bath time! Who cares if the margins are filled with spaghetti sauce fingerprints from the kitchen. And when you get interrupted in the laundry room, those fabric softener sheets make great bookmarks. Your Bible will smell good too!

God will honor you for trying to spend some time with Him during your busy day. Satan doesn't want you to find time to read your Bible. He knows that if you spend time in God's Word you'll become a powerful, victorious Christian. Just "bum Satan out" and take your Bible from room to room and read when you can! When you've finished reading Ruth, then return to this chapter.

• • • • • •

It was early in the cool, dark morning. Gently as possible, Ruth covered Naomi with a rough blanket and quietly made her way out of the house. Her legs cried out in pain as she made her way down the two crumbling steps outside their small home. She was discovering muscles in her back and legs that she never even knew she had, and all of them were sore! She looked down at her blistered hands, once delicate and smooth. She was grateful for the salve that Naomi, her mother-in-law, had lovingly massaged on them last night after she had returned from another day of gleaning.

Ruth decided that this morning she would pray as she headed west toward the barley field. She had often observed Naomi in prayer during the day, and she could see how that special time spent communing with Yahweh, the Almighty, was beginning to rejuvenate her dearest friend. She expected that if she too started her day talking to God, her attitude would become much better about doing the menial work that she was now forced to do for survival.

Ruth was truly grateful that she had decided to come to Bethlehem with her kind mother-in-law. She hurried along. Just as she was beginning to thank God for His kindness and protection, she was forced to move to the side of the road as a group of unkempt reapers, walking five abreast, brushed past her. The first rays of the morning light glinted from the sickles resting on their strong shoulders. Ruth took a second look at the man in the center. She caught her breath as she saw something in this handsome man that made her think of her late husband, Mahlon.

Ruth could not believe how much her life had changed! How it was turning out to be nothing like she had planned. She had been happy with Mahlon. They had had a good life in Moab. As she looked around at this new land in which she found herself, she wasn't exactly sure what God had planned for her, yet she was excited about the possibilities. One thing she was sure of was the "rightness" she felt in caring for Naomi. That was giving her deep satisfaction. She knew Mahlon would have wanted her to look after his mother. And yet Ruth was drawn to Naomi for a special reason, one having nothing to do with the wedding vows taken ten years ago.

Ruth stopped walking for a moment and dug into her shoulder bag for her breakfast—a ripe pomegranate. During the boring tasks of preparing meals, weaving baskets and drawing water, the elderly Naomi had shared her Lord with Ruth during those years in Moab. Naomi had made the old stories so interesting to young Ruth that she couldn't get enough of them. Chemosh, the god of the Moabites, could not compare; so naturally, when Naomi decided to leave and return to Israel, Ruth found herself pledging to go along and follow the God that had stolen both of their hearts.

The fresh spring breeze tugged and tried to pull Ruth's blue shawl from around her head. She was starting to feel better and less sore, now that she had walked a little while. She was not afraid of hard work and was not about to feel sorry for herself. Since the law of the land demanded that the corners of the fields not be harvested, to allow the poor and widowed to glean, *glean* she would! Ruth's mind raced, thinking of all the creative ways she would use the barley. She remembered the young mother next door who was always baking such wonderful smelling dishes. She decided she would stop by soon and ask her for some recipes.

Arriving at the field, Ruth joined the others as they made their way to its north corner. This was a different corner from before, but Ruth knew today would be much like yesterday—and the day before that, and well, like the last few weeks—hours of bending over and collecting the grain. She smiled, however, as she glanced around the perimeter of their corner and noticed that it backed up into a small brook. "During breaks, I'll put my feet into the cool water, and dip my shawl into it and place the cool cloth onto my forehead," she thought to herself. This got her through the boring day.

A nice surprise happened at the end of the day when she actually got to meet the man who owned the field, Boaz.

Naomi's wrinkled hand reached out and picked up the oil lamp from the table as she slowly made her way to the window. She stood there looking out at the inky night, digesting all the details that Ruth had just shared with her. Ruth, who was soaking her feet, turned in her wooden chair and looked at her mother-in-law, trying to read her body language. Because Ruth moved too quickly, warm water splashed out of the basin and onto the floor. Ruth was tired. She looked at her bed mat and blankets longingly. "Will it be sleep or a talk?" she wondered to herself.

Naomi finally turned and smiled. On her face—joy. "God is providing for us, Ruth. The man you met today, he is one of my 'kinsman-redeemers.' Why did I ever doubt? Where was my faith?" The old woman hugged herself and drew close to Ruth. "I did not recognize God's guiding hand, but now I see it—and it is more than a coincidence that you would end up in Boaz's field today, my dear Ruth. Bitterness has visited me and stayed too long since I lost my husband and my sons; I have moved away from God, Ruth, but He has never moved away from me." Naomi's old hands cupped Ruth's face. "God will honor you, my sweet Ruth, because of your faithfulness to me and your strong character. I forget sometimes what you have given up to follow me and my God, the God of Israel." Naomi knelt beside Ruth, and the two women bowed their heads. Blistered hands and wrinkled hands intertwined until they became one.

Naomi's prayer was quiet. She asked God to give them direction in what to do next, now that Ruth had met and received such favor from this kind man Boaz. She also prayed for Ruth and her future . . . for love, for children. Soon tears of peace and joy made their way down the faces of both women, a few falling onto their worn robes and finally intermingling with the small pool of water already around their feet. Water splashed from the basin, washing away the dirt and the grime of Ruth's long, hard day.

• • • • •

The story of Ruth has volumes to say to us mothers. In Ruth 2:7 we learn that Ruth had said to the foreman, "Please let me glean and gather among the sheaves behind the harvesters." To Boaz he later reports: "She went into the field and has worked steadily from morning till now, except for a short rest in the shelter." Gathering grain with other poor folks and old widows, does that sound exciting? It was the same task each day. Ruth had once had a husband and a life in Moab. Now, her husband was dead. She had left her homeland and everything she was used to in order to care for someone else.

Have you done that? Have you left a comfortable and exciting job to care for someone? I did and I'll never regret it! That "someone" is actually my three children and husband. Is it exciting to change diapers all day long? Is it exciting to clean the same house every week? To wash the same dishes? Hear the same Barney songs over and over? Fold your husband's underwear? No, these are menial jobs and beneath us—ahem!—but you know what? It is *God* who has blessed us with cute little kids, cozy but messy homes, and wonderful (for the most part) husbands, so let's take care of them faithfully. God will not forget what you've given up to care for your family. Just wait. God will not forget the sacrifices you are making.

He loves to reward the faithful and He will.

I feel a "rightness" about staying home and raising my children and caring for my family. The world, the media, and our modern culture will not threaten my "rightness." Don't let it do that to you either. This is our season to be home. Children are little for only a short time. Other moms may be taking their kids to day-care centers, but you don't have to follow the herd.

Ruth decided to be cheerful while she gleaned in the corner of the field. Instead of grumbling and complaining, she found the cool brook and the shade of the tree. While I'm here in this corner with diapers, bottles, and no time for myself, I'll look around and find something good, positive, and special in every day that God gives me with my family. I won't have to look very hard. God will provide it! Are you looking? Moms, He will honor us for our attitudes.

In verses 20 and 21 of chapter one we can sense the anguish in Naomi's words. "Don't call me Naomi," she told the people of Bethlehem, "Call me Mara, because the Almighty has made my life very bitter. I went away full, but the Lord has brought me back empty. Why call me Naomi? The Lord has afflicted me; the Almighty has brought misfortune upon me." Can we even grasp the pain that Naomi felt—losing a husband, and not one but two sons? I empathize with her and understand how she fell into the pit of bitterness and disappointment. She was sort of pushed, wouldn't you agree?

Naomi had failed to realize that God did provide opportunities for her. Her dark pit of despair contained a strong ladder. God had placed the ladder there for her, and each rung of the ladder was a promise from the heart of God. Dependable Ruth was up at the top of the pit, waiting on Naomi with outstretched arms. Ruth was ready to be Naomi's shadow, confidant, servant, and friend. The support was there; it just took Naomi a while to open her eyes to it. Do we let bitterness and disappointments blind us to the opportunities around us? Are supports available to us as struggling moms, yet we let them pass unnoticed? How can we forget that our God is a God of infinite resources? Yes, Naomi's economic security was gone, but she was enriched with love from a devoted daughter-in-law. Do we see our own riches?

If you return to the verse quoted earlier, it says that Ruth worked steadily but she rested in the shelter. As busy moms, our days go by in a blur. Can we multi-task or what? I'm going to encourage you to run to your "shelter" sometime during the day—even if it is for only 20 minutes. Your shelter is anything that you want to do. It must be relaxing for you. It could be reading a good book, watching a favorite TV show, walking with another mom in the neighborhood, or listening to a soothing CD. I know you "don't have time"! You must make the time for yourself. Don't feel guilty. Afterwards, you'll feel refreshed; and your kids and husband will benefit from your "shelter time" too. You'll be a happier mommy.

Lastly, this chapter of Ruth convicts me to keep on witnessing. We never know how our witnessing will affect another person's life, and possibly their future generations. Ruth was converted as an adult. She was not a Jew; she was a Moabite, a group of people often despised by the Jews. She grew up probably worshiping the god Chemosh. How fortunate for her that God brought Naomi, a strong believer, into her life to share His truth with her.

This is a wonderful illustration of how God doesn't have "favorites." Yes, God chose the Jews to be an example, but His plan was for all to come into the Kingdom. God didn't care that Ruth was of a different race and culture. She opened her heart to the Almighty. He came in "big time" and blessed her. God uses ordinary people. It's His style! Ruth's life had a purpose—and *your* life has a purpose. Raising little children is the highest calling.

How, in Ruth's wildest imagination, could she ever have known that she would become the great-grandmother of David, and an ancestor in the line of Jesus, the Messiah?!

Prayer of the Day

Dear Heavenly Father,

I admit that sometimes I am disappointed that the Bible doesn't have more stories about women. I know that the stories about men also apply to me and speak to the process of character building in all of us; yet as a woman I selfishly wish for more stories about strong women that lived long ago. Ruth lived in dark times, just as I do now. Her character and dedication stood out. What an example! Help me to see and appreciate the supports that You've placed in my life. And Father, thank You for these stories that topple the notion that spirituality is acquired through our race, our family tree, or other external factors. You see our hearts. Help me to make good choices with Your values and desires in mind. Even on the days when I feel my purpose in life is a complete mystery, I'll be steadfast and find my shelter in You. Amen.

Early Childhood Tip

My daughters always love to play "dress-up." Our costume box has seen more action than the toy chest ever did! Do you too have a daughter? Why not add a few Bible-character costumes to her collection of dresses? Stop by the fabric/craft shop and head straight for the clearance table. A few yards of beautiful material will make a gorgeous costume for any little girl wanting to be Miriam, Deborah or Ruth.

You could sew a simple tunic (for the base) or buy a plain, long nightgown or a long beach-coverup. Next, drape a yard or two of fabric for the layered look— think toga! For the headpiece you'll want to select a very lightweight fabric. An inexpensive crown or flowered candle wreath will hold the headpiece material in place. Next, stop by the ribbon section and choose some thick ribbon or decorative rope/braid trim to use as a sash for the waist. Complete the costume with a pair of inexpensive sandals and some gold or silver bangles for bracelets.

I think it is very important to share women of the Bible with our daughters but, at the same time, not limit them to role-playing just the characters found there. Encourage them to use their imaginations.

Ask: "What if David had a little sister along with him on the day he fought Goliath?" "What do you think they talked about?"

"Imagine all the things Mrs. Noah discovered about animals while organizing that ark!"

Encourage them to put themselves back in time!

This also provides a great "window of opportunity" where you can compare how women were viewed then and now. They'll be shocked at how women were frequently treated. Always underscore your talks with how kind and gentle Jesus was with women. Mary (His mother) was indeed precious to Jesus. Point out that Jesus chose to appear first to a woman, Mary Magdalene (a WOMAN!!!) on Easter morning, allowing her to be the one to announce His resurrection to the disciples. I love the fact that Jesus did that! Mary Magdalene was such a devoted follower. I love the way He honored her with that very special moment.

As mothers we must teach our children that Jesus did not view women as unimportant, even though He lived in a culture and time that did. Visit your local Christian bookstore for children's books about women of the Bible. Some stores also sell dolls, videos and stickers about Biblical women.

Chapter 9

A Deeper Relationship with Jesus

9

Wanted: Spelunkers - Apply Within

ONE day a father took his daughter to the mouth of a cave. He left her there and told her that he would one day return for her. She trusted him explicitly as he handed her a light, hugged her tightly and then left. Many years later, a wise man came by the cave and found the woman by the mouth of the cave. She looked tired and anxious. The old man asked if he could rest and enjoy the coolness of the cave for just a few minutes. After he caught his breath, he asked the woman to tell him about the cave. He was curious as to how deep it was, and if it contained any of the beautiful stalactites and stalagmites like the cave that he occupied. The woman looked unconcerned into the dark recesses of the cave and shrugged her shoulders. "I don't know anything about this cave," she replied. Surprised, he leaned forward and asked her quietly, "How long have you been here, woman?" She looked at him and said, "It has probably been twenty years or more, sir. I was a young girl when my father brought me here."

Before he could ask his next question, she began to complain about the conditions that she had been enduring over the years. She reported that horrible rain had often drenched her skin and clothes, and sandstorms had stung her eyes. Tears welled up in her blue eyes as she described her fear of the bats that left the cave on their nightly forays, only to return again. She pulled her robe up slightly to show the man her feet and ankles, blue and purple from bruises she had suffered from getting too close to the edge and falling down to the hard, rocky platform right beneath the cave's mouth. She told him that every time she stumbled and fell, it was extremely difficult to crawl back up to her original position.

She would have continued on with her list of complaints, but the wise man stepped forward and sat down very close to her and covered her lips with his old, crooked finger. "Woman," he said softly but with authority, "your father brought you here, yes?" She nodded, looking deep into his eyes. "He did not plan for you to stay at the mouth of the cave. He always meant for you to go deeper. There are riches inside for you to enjoy. This is a shelter to protect you until he returns for you." He removed his finger from her lips and pointed to the inside of the cave. The woman wept. He gathered her up into his arms, stroking her hair with his large hand. She understood and kissed him gently on his cheek, and finally walked into the cave.

Are we like this woman?—Christians who have trusted the Lord and been saved, yet while waiting for Him to return find ourselves stagnant in our spiritual walk? Are we living unprotected at the mouth of our cave, enduring the storms of life but never learning from them? Are we grumbling and complaining about the conditions around us? Do we trust ourselves too much where sin and certain temptations are involved? Do we get too close to the edge, and end up with bruises from falls and backsliding? Do we fail to understand why we stumble? Are we allowing Satan's daily attacks to swoop around us like bats, creating fear, worries and spiritual paralysis? Do we love our Savior, yet find that we're trying to do things in our own strength? We possess the light, but do we use it to journey and discover what is inside the refuge of the cave? Or are we at the exact place in our spiritual walk that we were when we were saved, having never gone deeper?

I can write this little story and ask these questions because I've been there. I'm guilty of all the things I've mentioned. I was that woman at the mouth of the cave. But I don't want to be her anymore. Nor do I want to have bruised feet from getting too close to the edge and falling into the same old sins. I'm tired of letting Satan swoop around me and take away my peace and joy. I'm fed up with letting the world beat me up and discourage me. Jesus died for me so I could have eternal life, but that is not all: He died to give me victory here—today—for all of my days, or until His return. He left you and me at the mouth of the cave, well-supplied with His light.

I'm going deeper into the cave. Are you coming too? Our eyes must adjust, our spirits must become quiet. Do we notice the commotion of the world and how it is getting fainter as we travel deeper? Our eyes, instead of constantly seeing problems, now see God's miracles—stalactites and stalagmites. Instead of complaining about the damp and wet conditions inside the cave, we'll be appreciative of the pools of clear, living water that are abundant all around us.

Occasionally the pathway ahead may divide and difficult decisions will have to be made. The world tells us to rely on ourselves, but we've failed in that and are now learning to rely on God. The light that He gives us will call attention to Satan's lies and give us discernment to navigate the difficult passageways found in this spiritual walk. The path may taper, some places becoming so narrow that we'll be forced to crawl on our bellies in order to continue. Quite a humbling position. Sometimes we'll wonder if we will be able to make it through the difficult passageways at all. The walls will appear to be closing in on us. Quitting will enter our minds for a split second. But do we really want to head back to the mouth of the cave? We were so exposed and unhappy there! Let us hold our ground and not give up the distance we've already covered.

Moms, Jesus knows how frail we are. Our stubbornness and occasional rebelliousness doesn't surprise Him in the least. Jesus will always be there to take our hand and guide us. Caves heighten our other senses because we can't rely on our sight to see far ahead. So, too, our faith will be heightened the deeper we go in our personal relationship with Jesus Christ. We'll rely on the indwelling Holy Spirit. And Jesus will be walking each step beside us as we become the imperfect but cherished "spelunkers of God"—cave explorers.

Scripture to read and meditate on today:

1 Samuel 23:26 through 24:22:
   Illustrates how David used a cave as a refuge. Notice how Saul rested at the mouth of the cave. David and his men were safe and unnoticed deep within the cave.

1 Kings 18:4
Obadiah hides 100 prophets (who were still true to the Lord) in two caves.
Revelation 6:15
In the end times, men will be terrified and flee to the caves, hoping to hide deep within. Interesting. See also Isaiah 2:19.

Prayer of the Day

Dear Heavenly Father,

Forgive me if I've tarried at the mouth of the cave too long. Guide my steps. Help me to keep making steady progress as I delve into a deeper relationship with You. Let me have courage, like the wise man in the story today. Help me to tell others that they don't have to be beat up by the world and Satan, but instead You've provided a refuge in a personal relationship with your Son, Jesus. Amen.

Early Childhood Tips

ROAD TRIP!!!

Why not take a little weekend trip and visit a cave? You'll want to visit one that is commercially maintained and safe. Do a little research and find the closest cave in your area of the country. Luray Caverns in Virginia is absolutely beautiful. Not only can you and your kids become "spelunkers" for a day, but you can drive on the famous Skyline Drive to view breathtaking vistas, or hike on the mountain trails. My children were all over the age of five when we visited our first cave. If you prepare them well, they'll enjoy the incredible experience that only a cave can provide.

* For more information contact—the Shenandoah Valley Travel Association, P.O. Box 1040, New Market, Va. 22844; Phone: (540) 740-3132. Or visit www.shenandoah.com.

* Luray Caverns—Phone (540) 743-6551 or write Luray Caverns, P.O. Box 748, Luray, Va. 22835. Or visit www.luraycaverns.com.

* For information on peak fall foliage times and fall-related events, call (800) 843-9873.

Chapter 10

Serving and Fruits of the Spirit

10

Am I Bearing Fruit or Am I Just Fruity?

I STRAIGHTENED my paper bib for the fifth time, trying to keep it from creating a paper pouch around my chin. My dentist was behind me, looking at my x-ray, and I could tell (he had stopped humming) that I had a cavity. I rebuked myself for having put off my appointment for so long. My dentist asked the ridiculous question, "Do you want novocaine, Liz?" He could tell by the immediate jingling sound of my bib chain that my answer was clearly "YES!!!" so he began preparations for my shot.

That evening at home, I became a little worried because the numbness was not wearing off. Now I have had novocaine before; the slurred speech, the expected "lost lip feeling" and the occasional attractive drooling I was familiar with, but not the unending numbness in my tongue. I didn't eat anything that night for dinner because, well, what was the point? Promptly the next morning I dialed the number of my dentist. As I hung up the phone, I sat down and tried to digest what he had just shared with me. The doctor told me that the feeling should come back, but it could take a few weeks . . . and there was a slight chance that the nerve was hit directly, in which case my sense of taste might never return!

I tried to look on the bright side. I imagined myself losing some weight while waiting for my taste buds to revive. After all, it's pretty easy to turn down lemon squares and cookies when they taste like wood chips. Oh, by the way, this nerve thing rarely happens when people are given novocaine, so don't use this as an excuse to miss your "pearly whites" appointment. It most likely won't happen to you. I'm just good at this kind of thing.

What made it especially difficult is that this dental nightmare happened in July. The farmer's fruit stand near my house was filled with baskets of red ripe tomatoes and sweet Silverqueen corn, and I couldn't enjoy any of them. This was really bad timing! This was my favorite "tasting season." It was also snow cone time! It's a Smoot summertime weekly ritual that I had to grudgingly let pass while everyone else enjoyed the scrumptious flavors.

I was getting very depressed as the few days turned into weeks. I prayed for healing and patience. I fought against self-pity. Yes, I couldn't taste; but others face real physical problems their entire lives. Well, the body is an amazing thing and it did repair itself, but it took three months for my sense of taste to return.

By then the ripe cantaloupes (which I dream about all winter), were gone. The snow cone shack was boarded up, a big "Closed for the Season" sign nailed to it. Gone were the sweet cherries from my dad's orchard; only the garnet stains at the bottom of the buckets remained. Needless to say, the by-product of this ordeal was that I learned to appreciate my sense of taste.

The fruit the following summer was extra delicious to me. This incident happened to me years ago, but I still truly anticipate the summer fruits and their enjoyable flavors with extra appreciation. I'll never take them for granted. Never!

Regardless of the season, there is some fruit that we should constantly desire in our lives. It's called the "Fruit of the Spirit." It's the by-product of a changed life and one that lives for God.

Galatians 5:22
The fruit of the Spirit is love, joy, peace, patience, kindness, goodness, faithfulness, gentleness and self-control.

When we cooperate with the Holy Spirit and surrender our will, these fruits are evident in our lives. Others should know who we follow by the fruit that we bear. I know what this fruit looks like; I've seen it. Many of the counselors that I volunteer with at the Billy Graham Telephone Ministry Center in Baltimore are heavy-laden with fruits of the Spirit. During the last ten years I've been blessed to be able to serve God and have made many precious friendships in the process. These counselors—men and women of all ages, races, and many denominations—manifest the patience, kindness and love of Christ as they converse with callers from all over the country. Viewers watching the Billy Graham telecasts are invited to call and speak to someone about accepting Jesus as their Savior, or to just have someone pray for them. People are truly hungry for a personal touch from God. Imperfect but loving volunteers connect with them and share God's love.

I believe that when you volunteer in any ministry, you follow Christ's example—you become a servant, and in the process God blesses you with a deeper revelation of Himself. Volunteering is like arriving at the orchard ready to work. There is much to do, and the sun is hot. As you roll up your sleeves to work, the Master of the orchard gently pulls you aside, brings you over into the shade of one of His fruit trees, and plucks off a delicious piece of fruit for you to enjoy. Then the Master begins to reveal just a few of the secrets of His magnificent orchard. By volunteering you think that you'll help others—and you do—but you get back so much more that you never expected. Well, the Lord is still working on me. I wouldn't say my branches are full of fruit yet . . . I'm more like a small fruit salad at the moment.

As you can see from reading the scripture above, the fruits produced by the Spirit jibe with the laws of Moses. God gave us the Law *and* sent us the Spirit. We can't have the fruit without linking our lives with the Holy Spirit. It's futile to try to get this fruit—peace, self-control, etc.—on our own. Yes, people do try. But we will definitely start to get "fruity" if the Bible, God's Word, pervades our minds; if God's love is behind the stuff we do; and if the Holy Spirit's power is welcomed within us, enabling us to grow in our spiritual walk.

There are always by-products of our life experiences. Always. So what do you think the by-products of being a stay-at-home mom will be for you? There will be so many! All of my children are in school now and I have to admit that I've recently been reflecting on the benefits of having stayed at home. By the time your children climb the school bus steps, you'll add many of your own to this list.

First, you will have no feeling of guilt. Secondly, you will have a special closeness with your children that only time and God's anointing can give you. Thirdly, you will have the opportunity to deepen your relationship with the Lord. You can rely on Him and allow Him to teach you about the joys of motherhood. An appreciation of your husband's sacrifices will grow deep in your heart. And, you'll surely look at future paychecks in a whole new light after such a long hiatus! Lastly, there will be a sense of pride in yourself. By sharing yourself and God's values with your children, you'll have given them an excellent start. God calls us to be women of excellence. Use this time wisely. And have no doubt: He will honor you for your choices!

Honestly, if we're not bearing fruit then we're standing still or backsliding. I know this because I was standing still for a while. I was "saved"—I knew I was going to heaven; but I wasn't maturing spiritually. Then God put a lot of things in my life—circumstances to rectify that situation. So if you are facing trials or feel that God is working on you about a certain area of your life, consider that a good sign. It means He is chasing you with His holy pruning shears. They hurt, as He tries to remove things from our lives that are keeping us from bearing the delicious fruit He knows we can bear. Pruning must be done so that the tree can grow and produce fruit. Well, God seems to think we need pruning, and He is right! He may be trying to prune selfishness, pride, jealousy and some other unhealthy habits and attitudes out of your life.

Believe me, it was sad not to taste fruit for a long summer season. But it's even sadder for our Creator when He sees us live a life without bearing fruits of the Spirit the entire season of our earthly lives.

Prayer of the Day

Heavenly Father,

Thank You for the wonderful gift of love that I can experience through Jesus and the Holy Spirit. I know that You did not intend for me to keep this love to myself, so please help me to show it and share it through the fruits of the Spirit. I sometimes fall short. I become impatient, lose my peace and relinquish self-control. May the Holy Spirit help me grow up in the areas where I need to mature.

It's hard to look at myself, but I desperately need to. I want the fruits of the Spirit: joy, peace, kindness . . . all of them!!! Not so that others will think well of me, but that You may be glorified. May I continue to learn from the interesting trials You put in my path. Lord, I'm thinking specifically of how amazing our senses are and the enjoyment that we can experience through them. Thank You. To be able to taste is such a blessing—one of the million blessings You sprinkle before me every day of my life, and I rarely acknowledge them. I'm pushing ahead, and every day I hope I become a "fruitier" Christian! Amen.

Early Childhood Tip

The "fruit smoothies" below should add some variety to your kids' snack time. They provide some calcium and vitamins too! *Bon appetit!*

• Peanut Butter-Banana Breakfast Shake •

½ cup frozen nonfat vanilla yogurt
⅓ cup skim milk
1 medium banana, broken into 4 pieces
1 tablespoon peanut butter

Place all ingredients in a blender jar. Cover and blend at LIQUEFY until smooth, about 20-30 seconds. Yield: 2 drinks. (Nutrition per serving: About 146 cal, 7 g pro, 22 g car, 4 g fat, 2 mg chol, 92 mg sodium.)

*Note - This is called a breakfast shake, but my kids enjoy it as an afternoon "pick-me-up"! I add a dash of vanilla and use whole milk, as it is a great way to get my son, a non-milk drinker, to absorb some calcium.

• The Apple Moo–Moo Smoothie •

1 3/4 cups milk
1/2 of a 6 oz. can of frozen apple juice concentrate
1 cup vanilla ice cream or vanilla frozen yogurt
1/2 tsp. cinnamon
a dash of vanilla

Combine the apple juice and the milk. Cover and blend 30 seconds. Next add ice cream, cinnamon and vanilla, and blend for 1-2 minutes until smooth. Yield: 5 (6 oz.) servings.

Okay, now when the kids are down for a nap, return to the kitchen and make the smoothie below for yourself! Enjoy!

• Spiced Peach Energy Drink •
(for rejuvenating Mommy's energy)

1/2 cup low-fat buttermilk (I use vanilla yogurt)
1/4 cup skim milk
1 can (8 oz.) sliced spiced peaches, packed in fruit juice, chilled and well drained
2 tsps. wheat germ
2 tsp. honey
a dash of cinnamon and nutmeg (I also add a dash of vanilla)
3 ice cubes

Place all ingredients except ice in blender jar. Cover and blend at STIR until smooth, about 10 seconds. Add ice cubes. Cover and blend at LIQUEFY, pulsing 3 to 5 times, about 3 seconds each time, until slushy. Yield: 1 drink. (Nutrition per serving: About 193 cal, 9 g pro, 37 g car, 2 g fat, 6 mg chol, 152 mg sodium.)

* The Peanut Butter-Banana Breakfast Shake and Spiced Peach Energy Drink are from the *Kitchen Aid 5-Speed Ultra Power Blender Instructions and Recipe Book*. P.O. Box 558, St. Joseph, MI 49085-0558

Chapter 11

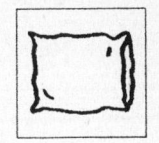

Saul

11

Patience

GRAB your Bible and turn to 1 Samuel 13:1–13. I know you are probably thinking I'm crazy asking you to read such a long passage today, but stick with me. This is a true story about Saul. I'll wait for you. Okay, here we go. Samuel told the Israelites that Saul was to become their king. Saul was a brave young soldier. Boldness and attitude were his middle names. Respect for him grew with each victorious battle, and men became excited about following him. He was becoming a hero and had a very bright future ahead of him. The Philistines were the strongest of Israel's enemies, and Saul and his men had to fight them often. Before one very important match-up with the Philistines, Samuel asked Saul not to begin the battle for seven days. Samuel said he would arrive on the seventh day and offer up a sacrifice, asking God to help them in this important battle. Meanwhile, Saul waited at Gilgal. Saul felt that Samuel was taking too long to reach him and his army. Many of his men were leaving. He panicked and decided to do things his own way, so he offered the sacrifice himself. Just as Saul was finishing the sacrifice, Samuel arrived. Excuses flew out of Saul's lips. Samuel called his action foolish and pointed out his disobedience in a major way. I'm sure Saul was not happy to hear that his future was altered forever. Amazingly enough, Saul won the battle that day against the Philistines, but he lost his kingdom.

Why did Saul take the shortcut? How could he have forgotten that an all-knowing, powerful God was in charge? Why couldn't Saul see that there was much more at stake than that little battle with another group of men? Was he blind to the futility of substituting ritual with real faith? Where was his patience? Why did he leave the protective care and wing of his Father, and strike out on his own? I ask myself these questions, too, in my own life. Why do I go for the shortcut, the easy way?

Saul saw some of his men leaving. The Bible doesn't say that all of them left. When we see our resources starting to dwindle, do we panic too? Do we look at what we have lost? Why not count and hold dear what we still have? Saul was a strong and brave soldier, remember? Where was his strong spiritual character, though? I imagine that Saul's men were privy to the fact that Saul had received the seven-day instruction. What a wonderful witness he could have been to those men who remained in the camp. He could have pulled them aside and said, "Listen men, I know things look bad and some of your buddies have left. The enemy is close and dangerous. But, I've got these instructions. It might sound crazy to wait, but we have to trust God's timing in this. I serve a mighty God. While we are waiting, let's pray, train and rest, okay?" Think of all the men who could have come to know God that day on the battlefield.

Every day we are on a battlefield ourselves. Satan tries to entice us to take the shortcut. When money gets tight, we'll want to stop giving. When we're exhausted, we'll want to curl up in our sheets on Sunday morning and skip church. When we are pressed for time, we'll stop reading the Bible. When the kids are driving us crazy, we'll give in and fail to discipline wisely. When our husband gets on our last nerve, we'll choose to spend time alone or retreat instead of working things out. This "obedience thing" is hard! Let's not take the easy way out. Let's do what God tells us in our spirit to do. It may seem crazy. Many times, we'll want to scream, "God, why are You taking so long to help me with this? Why won't You tell me what You want me to do? Why is this so hard?" Let's make a pact, you and I (remember we're in this motherhood thing together). Let's decide to keep all shortcuts in the kitchen with our recipes and not in our spiritual walk, okay?

Prayer of the Day

Lord, thank You for the old stories. They teach me truths and show me what to do to avoid problems. Help me not to be short-sighted, like Saul. He had such potential. I have potential too. Help me to be strong spiritually. My spiritual muscles are pretty weak right now, but I desire a change. Let me remember that there will be punishments when I take shortcuts. You are a loving God, but I know You require my obedience. This flesh is strong, but, Lord, I don't want to miss out on all the blessings You have planned for me!

Early Childhood Tip

My hometown had at least 15 museums within the town limits. What about yours? Okay, I guess my hometown is a little unique. I grew up just 10 minutes outside of Gettysburg, Pennsylvania. I grew up with the notion that a museum on every corner was a normal thing. I enjoyed touring them as a young girl and even worked at one during the summer.

When you go to a museum you can experience through the exhibits what something was once like. One purpose of history museums is to provide profitable lessons for future generations. Hopefully, people can look at these exhibits and learn how to avoid similar conflicts and problems in the future. The Bible is a museum of prose and poetry with a similar purpose. The Bible is overflowing with stories depicting love, strength, heroism and weakness.

Why not make a Bible museum of your own with your children? After you share a Bible story with your children, ask them to draw a picture about the story on a sheet of paper in a new notebook labeled "Our Bible Museum." If they are really young, a picture alone will suffice. You can label it and on the back write a brief summary of the story and the lesson you have learned. If your children are older, the picture can be much more elaborate and they can write the summary. Be creative. They may want to write it from a museum curator's perspective: "At this stop on our tour, you see a man named Saul . . . ." At the top of each page, remember to write the scripture where the story is found.

Later, when you have quite a collection of "exhibits" (pages with stories and pictures), you can challenge your kids by having them place the picture pages in the correct order using their Bible's Table of Contents page as a reference. This will help them to remember the Bible stories and where they are found. You might even want to make Old Testament museum pages one color and the New Testament pages a different color. Each page could list the name of the story, the characters, a brief summary, and a lesson learned from the story.

Eventually, you might want to add your family "Bible Museum" to the bookshelf in your den. It will be a museum that your children can "tour" anytime they want.

Chapter 12

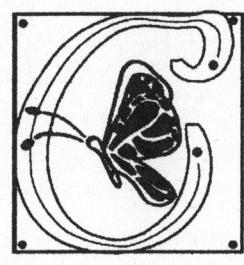

An Approachable God

12

Curtains

Matthew 27:51: *At that moment the curtain of the temple was torn in two from top to bottom.*

WE HAVE moved numerous times during our sixteen years of marriage. Unfortunately for my husband, we are in a new place for only a very short time before I begin to bug him about helping me to put up the curtains. I can't help it! Somehow those yards and yards of fabric dangling near the glass panes warm and soften the rooms. And somehow, on some level, pulling the curtains shut after a long, hard day gives the day closure for me. At times that closure is especially welcome—like after a trying day when the baby is cutting a tooth, the garbage disposal has broken (again), and I have eaten six chocolate chip cookies when I promised myself two.

In the 26th and 36th chapters of Exodus, we learn about a special curtain found in the Jewish tabernacle and later in the temple. It was there not to decorate or soften the temple, it was there to separate. Two sacred rooms, the Holy Place and the Most Holy Place, were separated by a beautiful heavy curtain made of blue, purple and scarlet yarn. Cherubim (angels) were depicted on the curtain, placed there by fine craftsmen. Daily the priest would enter the Holy Place and trim the lamps of the golden lampstand—the menorah. The smell of incense was strong in the Holy Place, for morning and evening incense was burned on the Altar of Incense, to denote unfading prayer. Twelve loaves of bread rested on the small golden table across from the menorah. Each Sabbath the priest would bring twelve fresh loaves to replace them.

However, only the high priest could enter the Most Holy Place, the Holy of Holies. Sounds a little intimidating, don't you think? This perfect cube-like curtained room contained the presence of God and the Ark of the Covenant. One day a year, on the Day of Atonement, the high priest would enter and make atonement for the sins of the people of Israel by sprinkling sacrificial animal blood. No one else could enter into the presence of God.

Immediately after Jesus died on the cross, something happened at the temple. That heavy curtain was torn in two from top to bottom. See Matthew chapter 27. Now the barrier between God and man was gone. No longer would God's children have to go through priests to reach God. No longer would sacrifices have to be laid at the altar. God wanted us to love and accept His Son as the perfect sacrifice, the perfect Lamb.

It's easy to be around approachable people, isn't it? They smile. Their body language shows an openness that puts you at ease immediately. They listen. They are patient. They are gentle. They are kind. Who does this sound like? Does it sound like Jesus? If God was trying to show us through Jesus that He was an approachable God, then I think God did an amazing job. People wanted to be around Jesus. Many Jews and Gentiles walked miles and endured the elements to get just a glance at Him. Jesus was approachable. By tearing the curtain in two God was clearly saying, "Come near. Didn't you see Me in My Son? I'm approachable, I care about you, I want a relationship with you."

The curtains you choose for your dwelling place tell a lot about your personality. I've found that just looking at all the hundreds of window decorating ideas available can make a person dizzy. I checked out a book about window treatments from the library; I was exhausted by the time I made it to chapter two. The pressure of choosing between a gathered valance and bishop-sleeve draperies with sheers, or between the rod-top draperies with multiple bow ties and Roman shades, just became too much for me! What curtain did our heavenly Father choose for His holy dwelling place? Did He choose blue and purple because they are colors of royalty? Was the scarlet color there to foreshadow the blood of Christ? Why angels on the curtains? Were they portrayed there in an attitude of worship to indicate the holiness of the One dwelling within?

I put up curtains to feel "at home." But Jesus Christ tore down the curtain to show us the way *to* our home. Somehow there was closure.

> *The holy partition of purple and blue*
> *Was torn in half for me and you;*
> *God remained holy, but beckoned us in—*
> *A cross and a Son erasing our sin.*

For additional meditation - See
> *Exodus 26*
> *Romans 3:25*
> *Hebrews 9:24–28* (If you only have time for one today, try to read this one!)

Prayer of the Day

Dear Heavenly Father,

Jesus stood in my place. He gave Himself so that I could have access to You. That is so amazing. That day on Calvary, many things changed forever . . . Your temple, Your church, Your people, Your covenant. Thank You for showing us through Jesus that You are approachable and that You desire a closeness with us. I'm thankful for that ripped curtain. It's an invitation. Will we come? When curtains are put up, there is separation and darkness. Now that the veil is split, we are together and there is a great light. Help me to keep seeking that light. Amen.

Early Childhood Tip

In 1 Chronicles 22:5 David tells us that, though he was not permitted to build God's temple, he would help with preparations and his son Solomon would carry out the task. David said, "My son Solomon is young and inexperienced, and the house to be built for the Lord should be of great magnificence and fame and splendor in the sight of all the nations. Therefore

I will make preparations for it."

The children of Israel followed God's directions carefully when they constructed the temple. The early childhood idea today is a "following directions" game. Play this game with your children to help prepare them for school. It is a game to foster listening skills. As a teacher, I can't stress enough the importance of good listening skills. By playing this game you'll encourage little ears to hear 1-, 2-, and 3-step directions. Your children will enjoy playing this game regularly. I know mine did!

When your child enters a structured school setting, his or her teacher will constantly be giving them 2- and 3-step directions. She may say, "Class, put your name on your paper, place it in your reading folder and get in line for Science." That is a lot for little ears and brains to remember. That is why it is so beneficial to train them early. You can help them develop this important skill. Following directions is not only a valuable "school skill," but it's also a lifetime skill.

Use my angel pattern (see pages 222-223) to trace or draw ten purple, ten blue, and ten red angels (the colors found in the temple curtain). You can use construction paper or poster board. Cut the angels out and with a black magic marker add on the angelic features. Group your blue angels together. They will be the Easy Set—1-step direction cards. Turn them over and write the following directions on the back of the blue angels. Each angel gets one direction only.

* walk to a window
* touch a chair
* say a fruit
* jump in the air
* touch your neck
* shout a friend's name
* give someone a hug
* touch your knees
* turn around quickly
* touch something blue

Next, collect all of your purple angels. This will be your set of 2-step direction cards—Medium Level. Turn your paper angels over and write these directions on the back.

* walk to the couch and clap your hands
* sit down quickly and say a color
* knock on a door and whisper your name
* walk three steps and sing a song
* lie on the floor and touch your nose
* say a number and touch your toes
* kiss someone on the cheek and stomp your feet
* touch a closet door and name a day of the week
* spin around two times and name an animal
* run to a window and tiptoe back to Mommy

Now that you have the knack, prepare the red cards yourself. You know your kids better than anyone. You can tailor-make the cards to suit your home and your child's interests. For example, you might write: Point to Fluffy's water bowl, touch the kitchen phone, and sit on Daddy's chair. The red cards are the Challenge Cards. Each red card will have a 3-step direction on it. It will take some time for your kids to be able to do the red cards, but they'll enjoy the challenge! If you are excited about the game and encourage them, they'll be excited too! You might want to make some of the cards funny. My children loved the cards that told them to snore or sneeze!

I hesitate to suggest age appropriateness on some of these activities because every child is different. You know what your child can handle. Go slowly.

Store your angel cards in a set of cute tins or in large envelopes. You could draw angels on the envelopes or buy angel stickers to place on the front of each envelope or tin. Label them "Angel Listening Game."

Place the blue angels in a wide tin, facing up; or take them out of the envelope and place them on the floor in a small pile. Mix the angels and invite your child to choose one. My kids loved to close their eyes and reach in and grab one. They hand the angel to you and you read the directions carefully and slowly. Then they do the direction. At the beginning say the direction two times. Later, progress to only once. Praise them. If they forget a step, say, "I know it is hard to remember sometimes, so listen and I'll repeat it." Make sure your child looks at your face and is "tuned in" before you start the direction.

Once they are completely comfortable with the blue set, introduce the purple set. And ultimately the red set. I always kept the Easy and the Medium Sets in their respective tins, so that if the children wanted to choose an easier card sometimes (and they will) they have the option. They will be comfortable with the blue set, yet will want to challenge themselves with the new purple set. And likewise with the red set. This is why we make the sets in different colors—so that they can have some control.

Remember to praise them. If they do one part of the direction but forget the other part, say, "That's okay, you did part of it. I'm proud of you. I'll give you a hint about the second (or third) part."

For some variety, tell your children that today you are going to say the direction one time only. Watch those little ears perk up!

Did you happen to notice that on two of my cards I have the direction "kiss someone" or "hug someone." When you are a stay-at-home mom, YOU always get to be the SOMEONE!! Mmmmm . . . life is good.

Chapter 13

Discipline/Training

13

Out of Booties and Into Boot Camp!

*I*F THEY were to dress for the part, your little children would be dressed in green khakis from age one through six. Come to think of it, so would you! Training camp is about to begin. And the battle is a battle of wills. Oh, don't worry, it won't be quite as strict as boot camp. You won't play reveille at 0600 or anything like that. Instead, you'll probably hear, "Won't You Be My Neighbor?" by Mister Rogers. And relax—your troop will get lots of "leave" at the playground down the street. As long as you remember that you are the General and they are the privates, you'll not only survive boot camp but you'll finish it with joy and satisfaction.

Proverbs 22:6 tells us to . . . "Train a child in the way he should go, and when he is old he will not turn from it." When you train someone, it takes a tremendous amount of time and energy. This is our responsibility as parents. It is not the babysitter's, the day-care's, or the school's. It is ours. There will be a "season" when the kids are between one and three years old when you will feel that your entire day was spent on scolding and disciplining your children. "Don't touch!", "Please stop that!" and "No!" will be spilling out of your mouth so regularly that you'll seriously consider recording these commands onto a cassette tape. But don't give up! Please stand firm! This "season" will pass. Oh yes, you'll always be disciplining; but in time, you'll find that you're passing out fewer punishments and enjoying your children more. Hang on!

Have wisdom. *Wisdom* is doing today what you'll be happy and content with tomorrow and in the years to come. Do you want children who listen and respect you and other adults? Do you want children that have good manners and think of others? Then get ready for some work. This will not just happen! I wish it could be so easy. Many people just surrender (raise the white flag) and give in to the demands of their children. They don't want to deal with the battle of the moment.

During our lives, all of us have been in some sort of training. For instance, it could have been training for a degree, a job, or a sport. Quality training involves several steps:

1) Training is intense. It is sometimes painful, hurting both the trainer and the trainee.
2) Training involves submitting to and respecting authority.
3) Training has clear objectives. These objectives rarely change.
4) Training is preparing one to be on one's own and able to handle the job independently at a future date.
5) Upon completion of the training, both parties experience pride and satisfaction.

Think about these components as you train your children.

Hebrews 12:11 (TLB)
Being punished isn't enjoyable while it is happening—it hurts! But afterwards we can see the result, a quiet growth in grace and character.

It is difficult to discipline your children, but if you love them you will. When Johnny has a temper tantrum and crys and screams his demands, you must remember to hold your ground. If you give in to his demands, you are teaching him that if he has a temper tantrum he will get what he wants. You are reinforcing bad behavior, and you will pay for it for many, many years. Instead, cup his cute little face in your hands and say, "Mommy is going to totally ignore you while you are screaming like this. I said *no* and I *mean* no! I will talk to you when you've decided to calm down." Then walk away from him and ignore him. Go about your day and act as if he were invisible. He may cry for a while, but eventually he'll figure out that his behavior did not cause you to act the way he was hoping you would.

When a red-faced, soggy, temper-tantrum culprit crawled into my lap later, I would say, "I'm glad you decided to calm down. Let Mommy tell you why I had to say no to you. (Explain.) I love you, but I do not like the way you were behaving and it is not acceptable!" Encourage your child to go on to another activity, and forgive and forget.

Believe me, at the age when they are manipulative enough to try the dreaded temper-tantrum tactic, they are old enough to understand your reaction (and eventually your words). My children tried temper tantrums a few times but I was steadfast, and they quickly learned it was only bringing them a sore throat from screaming and puffy eyes from crying.

And that is the point. After a few times of that, they'll discover temper tantrums won't get Mommy to do what they want. It's pretty clear cut. This particular boot-camp drill—dealing with temper tantrums—can be completed in a few short days . . . or twelve or more years.

When a situation presents itself where you must say no and your children don't have a temper tantrum, praise them profusely. "I love the way you reacted when I said no this time. You didn't cry and scream. I'm so proud of you. I know that you were disappointed that I had to say no, but you remembered how to handle it." I suggest giving a little reward. It could be reading an extra book before bed, a sticker, or extra time to play outside. After some time, a tangible reward will no longer be necessary. A positive comment and smile from you will be all that they need. They have always desired your attention, but now they are realizing that they can receive it and be rewarded for positive behavior! Remember, reward good behavior. Compliment your children when you catch them being good!

J. Philip Everson once said, "Mountaintops inspire leaders but valleys mature them."* Pregnancy and the thrill of a newborn is a magnificent mountaintop. You feel on top of the world and feel in many ways as if you're looking at life through fresh, new eyes. Now as your little baby matures and begins to explore his/her new world, you find yourself entering a valley. It's a time when the General in you must contemplate some sort of disciplinary strategy for the next few years—the early childhood years. It can be a valley or it can be a pit. I believe that you make that decision. Valleys mature us.

---

* Zig Ziglar, *Something Else To Smile About* (Nashville, TN: Thomas Nelson, 1999), p. 17.

Disciplining a young child is one of life's biggest challenges. But if you fail to discipline, your valley can turn into a deep, dark pit. You will be extremely frustrated because your kids will be driving you crazy; plus, they'll be out of control. When you are in a pit, nothing grows. No light can reach anything to make it grow. In a true valley there is an abundance of growth. Mistakes will be made, but your children will grow to love and respect you in this valley if you correct, inspire, and teach them in a way that is grounded in mutual respect and the love demonstrated to us by the light of Jesus.

You, as the General, have resources at your disposal to help you through these training years. God's Word is your manual. The Holy Spirit, in tandem with your own good common sense, is your guide. Don't forget to seek sound advice from "seasoned" mothers. They've been in the battle and have seen years of active duty. Why do we fail to go to the moms who have been in the trenches? Why are we so quick to adhere only to advice from educated men who have been working on their Ph.D.'s? Ask for advice from older moms that you respect. Find out what worked for them. Veterans could be your best resource.

Many mothers, in their hunt for resources, find themselves in front of library or bookstore shelves searching for the latest books on discipline. As a teacher, I strongly recommend educating yourself in advance, but be wary. Not all bestsellers, and not all psychologists, give advice that lines up with common sense or, more importantly, with the teachings of Jesus Christ. Seek good advice, but guard your mind and heart. If what you're reading doesn't line up with the New Testament and you feel "strange"—the words not clicking and making sense to you—it is the Holy Spirit giving you a "check." Respect that. This is the way God protects believers from untruths.

Some secular psychologists may indeed offer good suggestions and ideas about disciplining young children. However, read with a discerning heart. God's Word must be our final authority. Read, pray for wisdom, seek advice from experienced parents, and then, after collecting all that information and insight, ask God to help you make the best decisions. Don't sell yourself short. God gave you beautiful children. I think He recognized capable hands. As a stay-at-home mother of three, and a teacher (no Ph.D., but a purple heart for seeing lots of action), I strongly suggest the books by Christian psychologist Dr. James C. Dobson.* When I read his books and soaked in his ideas regarding children and godly parents, a good "check" happened in my heart. When we follow the advice of Christian psychologists and insightful followers, we receive advice and suggestions that are grounded on the "rock" of Jesus Christ, not the "sand" of the latest research and our fickle culture's newest trends.

Training should be a time of consistency. One of the most difficult times is when your little ones go from crawling to walking. They start to get into everything. Most of your pretty decorations need to be banished to the attic until the coast is clear of sticky little fingers. Decide on the rules of the house and stick with them. For example, I recommend that you baby-proof your home, but I suggest leaving a few decorations around. Instruct your toddler that these are "special" things. These items are not to be touched.

Once in a while, I would scoop up my toddler and walk around the house with him in my arms. I would say, "Mommy is holding you, so if I'm with you, you can touch our special things." Pick up the decorations and let him see and touch them. I remember my little ones thinking that this was so exciting! A few times during the week, they would run to me and ask for "special" time. This way they'll learn that some items are off limits. When you visit friends or family that do not have a completely baby-proof, sterile home, you'll feel comfortable, knowing that your children can handle a short visit without destroying the place. I believe in training them at an early age to have limits and boundaries.

Be consistent. I think the one-warning strategy works well. If my child was doing something inappropriate like throwing sand at the playground, I would quietly and calmly say, "Throwing sand can hurt someone's eyes. You need to stop that now." If he continued to throw sand, the one-warning strategy was employed. Tell your youngster, "If you don't stop, then we will have to leave the

---

* Best known for his *Dare to Discipline*—a classic. Dr. James C. Dobson is founder and president of Focus on the Family, a non-profit evangelical organization dedicated to the preservation of the home. "Focus on the Family," his radio broadcast, is heard on more than 2,000 radio stations. I urge you to tune in to it on your radio. You'll be blessed!

playground for today. This is your warning." If he throws the sand again, pick him up and go home. I know that is a hard thing to do. You were probably looking forward to getting some fresh air too. Oh, they'll scream and embarrass you. But, believe me, your child will quickly understand that when you give him or her a warning you will follow through.

Teach him that he, not you, made the decision to disobey. He'll learn that his decisions have consequences. Soon he'll start making better decisions, and be happier with the consequences! You can be sure that the next time you take Johnny to the playground and give him a warning, he'll obey. Why? Because you have demonstrated that you will follow through and take him home. If you give him a warning and then fail to follow through, you are showing your child that your warnings don't mean anything. Remember, you are in charge. If, on the other hand, he obeys when you give him the warning, and stops throwing the sand, praise him for obeying and give him a reward. Be sure to let him know how proud you are of him for listening and choosing to obey. Compliment! You might want to let him stay at the playground an extra ten minutes as a reward for the positive behavior. Compliment while being consistent.

My son, Hunter, at age three, must have felt he was in some sort of Olympic training for jumping on the couch. He would "train" while watching videos or favorite TV shows. When I saw him using the sofa for a trampoline, I would say something like . . . "Hunter, you need to stop jumping on the couch. You could fall and hurt yourself. The furniture was made to sit on, not jump on. This is your warning. If you decide to keep jumping, then the TV will be turned off. If you obey, perhaps we can go outside and do some jumping after your movie. It's your choice." If Hunter resumed his jumping, the video was turned off immediately. If, instead, he obeyed, I gave him a hug and a compliment. After the video, we went outside and set up some items in the yard for him to jump over or jump into.

Be tuned in to your children. If they like jumping, turn the negative into a positive. You don't want your kids jumping on the furniture, yet they need to develop those basic motor skills. You know what your kids enjoy. Use that as a guide when bestowing rewards.

Compliment! I know I sound like a broken record, but a compliment like "Hunter, you are such an awesome jumper. Mommy loves to see you jump outside or inside on the floor, but not on the couch, okay?" will leave him feeling good about himself, but recognizing appropriate times and places for his jumping.

As I write this book—this chapter—I'm enjoying comparing Christian principles with everyday things. You know, of course, that I'm just teasing by comparing your "season" of intense disciplining to boot camp. I certainly wouldn't want any mother to be as strict and inflexible as a real Army general must be with his troops. (I swear I've never seen a general kiss his troops—and I'm guilty of kissing my privates all day long!) What is awesome is when, as a Christian mom, you guide with a firm and loving hand. When done in combination with showing your children Jesus, something amazing begins to happen. Your children learn to listen and follow your and your husband's rules; but at the very same time, they begin to listen to a higher calling. They begin to desire better behavior in themselves because they are growing to know Jesus and want to love and honor Him. That transition is the main goal!

General Mom, I want you to take another look at your orders. You know the orders *you* received when you got this small troop. Yes, okay, we've just covered the first part of it. That was to "train the child. . . ." Good. That seems to be going well—let's say there's a work in progress. The second half is a little more difficult. Go on. Read it: ". . . and when he is old he will not turn from it." Yes, it assumes that one day the little soldiers will grow up and leave your ranks—march out into the real battle. Every day you bond with them; but you're really one day closer to when you must let them go. You must prepare them *and* yourself. Both elements of the order are necessary. A good general needs to follow through on both parts. A good general doesn't keep a capable soldier on the base forever.

But cheer up, moms. I know how you are feeling right now. When you have the privates tucked in at the barracks and the camp is finally quiet, your mind starts to replay all the things you said and did throughout the day. You feel, perhaps, as if you yelled, scowled, and gave out "time-outs" as freely as a cop giving speeding tickets on the interstate. I know you are weary. As you take off your "four stars"—I mean your earrings—you look in the bathroom mirror and you wish you didn't have to be so "mean." After all, they are just little and soooo cute. Hang on! They are loving you as you make them "toe the line." When you discipline children with love it translates into . . . "my Mommy loves and cares about me."

I close today with advice and encouragement from a REAL general. General Dwight D. Eisenhower once said, "Leadership is the ability to persuade others to do what you want them to do because they *want* to do it."*

Prayer of the Day

Dear Heavenly Father,

I sometimes wonder why You put us together this way. We scorn any kind of discipline or training. We want to go our own way, both as little children and as adults. We know in our heart of hearts that discipline is good for us, but we usually want the easy way out. Help me as I attempt to "train up" these little children you've given me. Give me the strength I need during this season of intense battle of the wills. Give me confidence. Bless me with generous amounts of patience. Show me the words and give me discernment so that I may discipline my children in a way that would be pleasing to You, Father. I get frustrated with my children when they make the same mistakes over and over. But why should I react like that? *You* continue to show favor and bless *me* when I continue to make the same mistakes over and over again!

Help me to appreciate the time I have with them now, because I know that the day will come when I'll look back on these days as not the hardest days, but . . . the best days of my life. Amen.

Scripture to read and meditate on today:

1. Titus 2
2. John 17:11
3. Proverbs 13:24
4. James 3:1–2
5. Ephesians 6:4
6. Philippians 4:13

* *Something Else To Smile About*, p. 33.

Early Childhood Tips

Tip 1. Be prepared. As you know, children wiggle a lot and need to change activities often. So whenever you go to a restaurant, don't forget to take your backpack. Your backpack could contain a plastic lunchbox filled with crayons, scissors and pencils. You'll possibly want to add coloring books, plain paper, picture books, word-search books, small travel games and small toys, too. A few snacks, like crackers and granola bars or raisins, could be placed in a small plastic bag for "munchie" emergencies. My backpack also has a small bottle of that new anti-bacterial gel which is perfect for little hands. While you're waiting for your meal, bring out activities one at a time. When you see that they're getting bored, bring out something new. Keep these toys in the backpack. If these items aren't a part of their everyday playroom scene, then they'll be more exciting to your youngsters. When you provide fun activities, you'll find that your discipline problems are drastically reduced.

Tip 2. Do you enjoy knowing what to expect when you go somewhere? Well, so do children. If you are going to church or a show and the children will be sitting with you, prepare them well. Tell them what you can about the program. Explain that it is a *sitting* time and that they'll not be allowed to wander in the aisles. Give them your expectations for their behavior. For example, "I expect you to be quiet during the show and to play with the things in your backpack. In the middle, there will be a break—it's called intermission—and then you'll be able to move around and we'll get something to eat and drink. I know you can be a good listener. If you need to talk to Mommy, you must use a whisper voice."

Compliment them when they are following your directions.

If they are in kindergarten, they'll be old enough to pay attention and watch the show, and should be encouraged to do so. If your child is younger than that, and you can't avoid taking him, then please provide something for him to do. You'll be happier, the child will be happier . . . and the other adults that sit close to you will be ecstatic!

Chapter 14

Reflecting Christ

14

A Splash of Transformation

HUDSON TAYLOR, a pioneer missionary to China, decided to use a prop one day to illustrate a point in his sermon. He filled a glass with water and placed it on a table in front of him. While speaking to the congregation, he pounded his fist on the table. The pounding was forceful enough to make the water splash onto the table. Afterwards, he explained, "You will come up against much trouble. But when you do, remember, only what's *in* you will spill out."

How do we respond to temptations and trials? What spills *out* of us? Do we let anger and frustration over problems ruin our day? Do we invite ourselves to a pity party and stay there for a few days? When we are misunderstood, do we punish our husbands or our children with the loooooooooonnnngggggg silent treatment all week? Do we get offended, and think and speak harshly of others? I spent so many years responding in this way. I was so stubborn and miserable. I still act this way, but not as frequently.

Think of the sweet, fresh milk that you put in your baby's bottle. It satisfies and gives nourishment. But did you ever misplace a bottle and find it a few days later? I'm sure the smell was foul when you finally discovered it and tried to wash it clean. I've left a couple of forgotten bottles in the diaper bag for a day or two! They were gross and sour! That was and *is* me (sour!) when I let my emotions stew for a few days, instead of handling things the way Jesus would want me to.

It's so easy to give in to our flesh. Our flesh definitely wants its own way. Satan wants us to listen to our "flesh"—our "old" self.

The "father of all lies" knows that if we are transformed we will grow in grace, and we will begin to react quite differently to trials that come our way.

Are you being tested right now? Well, if you are, relax; it is an open book test. God gives only open book tests. It took me a long time to realize this! All we need to do is to spend time getting to know and apply the Bible. I have had to take a lot of make-up tests. He seems to put me in study hall quite a bit too! But the good news is—the Bible has transforming power.

Who are we listening to? We must guard our hearts and minds. We must let the Holy Spirit take control of our lives. Only then will we begin to react to situations with patience, kindness and understanding. Will we still get angry and disappointed? Sure, of course; but we will begin to handle things differently, knowing that we are not in our struggles alone. Jesus goes through them with us. We finally learn, through experience, that a hard heart and rebellious attitude only bring us unhappiness and cripple our spiritual growth. And if we really think about it, those sour attitudes erode our Christian witness to our spouse, children and friends. They look at the water splashing out of us!

So what are we filled with? What would the water look like flowing out of us? Would it appear calm at first, but upon closer inspection show little ripples on the surface—of anger or resentment, maybe jealousy, negativity, and dark hopelessness? No more! We are transformed in Christ! Jesus is the "living water"—fresh and clear. This water makes us, His children, sparkle with hope, love, forgiveness, patience and power! That includes the power to change!

Scripture to meditate on today:

Mark 7:14–17

Again Jesus called the crowd to him and said, "Listen to me, everyone, and understand this. Nothing outside a man can make him 'unclean' by going into him. Rather, it is what comes out of a man that makes him 'unclean.'"

Ephesians 4:22–24

You were taught, with regard to your former way of life, to put off your old self, which is being corrupted by its deceitful desires; to be made new in the attitude of your minds; and to put on the new self, created to be like God in true righteousness and holiness.

2 Corinthians 3:18

And we, who with unveiled faces all reflect the Lord's glory, are being transformed into his likeness with ever-increasing glory, which comes from the Lord, who is the Spirit.

Prayer of the Day

Heavenly Father,

I'm pretty used to this "old" me. The "new" me will be a reflection of You, and so I desire it; but I'm scared and unsure of all the changes involved in this transformation. Give me a teachable heart. Lord, help me to stay on the potter's wheel while You mold and shape me. I must trust You. My flesh is so strong. I scream for my own way, pity myself, and allow Satan to get a foothold on my many weaknesses. Why can't I just calm down and remember who I am?—Your child. But a child who needs to grow up spiritually. I guess I just need to hang out with You more, Lord, so that this "changing stuff" will become easier—okay? Fill me up with lots of You! Amen.

Early Childhood Tip

Collect a few small mirrors. Take the mirrors and your children with you as you walk around your home. I suggest that you designate yourself as the "mirror holder" (for safety reasons) until you stop walking; then you can let each child hold a small mirror. Put your mirror close to a variety of objects and show your children that the image in the mirror is the reflection of the object.

For example, put a mirror under a houseplant leaf, under

the faucet, or beside one of their favorite toys. Be creative! They'll enjoy exploring and seeing the object, but with a different perspective.

Sit on the carpet with your children and face them. Invite them to look in the mirrors at their own reflection. Now, put the mirrors behind you or in a bag (so the children won't be distracted), and place your Bible in front of them. If the children have their own Bibles, then place their Bibles in front of them. (Age 4 or 5 is a good time to give them their own Children's Bible.)

Share with your children that God's Word, the Bible, teaches us about God's Son, Jesus. Jesus lived in a place called Israel, thousands of years ago. Jesus was a gentle, kind and loving man. He loved to tell everyone He met about His Father in heaven, God. Jesus tried to show people that God loved them. Jesus wanted the people to be happy and tried to show them a new way to think and act. Some of their old ways needed to be changed. Let's compare the old ways with the new ways that Jesus talked about.

Old Way
    Some of the people were very greedy.

New Way
    Jesus told them to share and give things away.

Old Way
    Some of the people were snobby. That means they did not include others (especially the poor and the weak).

New Way
    Jesus told them to love everyone, even the people that didn't like them or treat them well. Jesus wanted them to be humble and not to think that they were better than others.

Old Way
  Some of the people did not want to forgive others.
New Way
  Jesus told them to forgive others, over and over again.

It was very difficult for the people listening to Jesus to change their feelings and actions. They were so used to their old ways! But they believed that Jesus was wise and that He desired good things for them. They were beginning to admire and trust Him. Jesus wanted to help them to change.

Do you think Jesus forced the people to change? No, He did not. Jesus gave them a choice. Some people listened and tried to change, and Jesus helped them. This made them happy; and even when things in their lives were not going so well, the people were still peaceful. Some people, however, were stubborn and foolish, and they held onto their old ways. They were not happy. They never had any peace or joy. They missed out on many of God's blessings because they refused to let Jesus help them to change.

Ask: "When you looked into the mirror a few minutes ago, who did you see?

"You saw yourself, right?

"You are going to get older and bigger. But you'll always look in the mirror and see you.

"Do you know what God is hoping will happen as you get older?

"God is hoping that you will think and act more like Jesus. The outside of you will always look like you, but the inside, your heart, can begin to change and become more like Jesus. Jesus won't leave you to do this by yourself. He'll help you if you ask Him to. He wants you to be happy.

"When we held the mirror close to the plant a few minutes ago, did you see the reflection of the plant?

"When we held the mirror close to the toy train, did you see the reflection of the toy train?" (Replace "plant" and "toy train" with items that you observed on your "mirror walk.")

"Well, if you are a Christian, you'll become so close to God that you'll start to see the reflection of Jesus in *you!*"

Chapter 15

Exercise

15

A Workout

ARE YOU frustrated about your weight? Do you promise yourself that today is going to be the day you stick to your diet plan . . . only to screw up by late morning and feel guilty the rest of the day? Are you angry with yourself because you can't fit into your clothes? I have felt this way. You are not alone. I have had to watch my diet ever since I was in high school. I had three children in the space of five years. I know how difficult it is, being surrounded by food all day and being in charge of all the meals and snacks. It's easy to see how women, once they become mothers, start to lose the battle and begin to gain weight.

With each pregnancy, with each pound, I felt more and more like an old dog lying on the porch of a hillbilly's cabin. I was tired and worn-out. But I was just too lazy and unmotivated to stop eating all the good "vittles" I found in my bowl every day. I knew I had to fight back if I was going to return to my pre-pregnancy shape (or somewhere even remotely near it!). But losing weight is so hard!

In my Bible I have a chart that compares diligence and laziness. It says, "The diligent will reap abundance through hard work. The diligent will be fully satisfied." I knew working out was hard work, but I also knew I would be satisfied with the results. Plus, I would have more energy to do all the things God was calling me to do. Now the laziness part: it says, "The lazy experience poverty because of their laziness and are full of excuses." Ouch!!!! "The lazy man loves pleasure and becomes poor." I had an abundance of excuses. I'm too tired! I can't help the snacking! I have to keep this food in the house for the kids! I don't have time to go to the gym! Exercise is boring! I've tried before!

When we are overweight and out of shape, we sometimes feel self-pity, isolation, and just generally out of control. We keep trying to lose weight or start an exercise program, but keep failing.

Some of us struggle with this problem on our own, waiting for motivation. Others reach out to support groups or counselors. But do these groups really want to help us, or are they only going to offer to help as long as we keep buying their products or attend their classes? We do want and surely need companionship when we are going through trials. This weight thing is definitely a trial, and I bet you are tired of going to jail every day! Ask God to help you with this problem! Perhaps He's been waiting for you.

When my children have a project that must be completed for school, they usually come to me or my husband for help right away. They know that we will help them with the project. Will we do it *for* them? No! They must do the work—to learn. But we help them collect the materials they need to be successful with the project. Those supplies are usually in our craft cupboard at home. Time is set aside daily to get it done, because we know that anything worthwhile takes time. When my children whine and groan about all the hard work, I remind them that the finished project will be marvelous and belong to them! I'm sure this is similar to what you've experienced in your home with your own children.

Why not go to your heavenly Father right away for help with your project—losing weight and feeling better about yourself? The supplies you need are probably right there in your home... sneakers, weights, and workout equipment (collecting dust?). You must set aside time! Why is it so easy for you to give time to everyone else and not yourself? You will whine and groan, too—I'm sure of it. But, through prayer and hard work your project will start to take shape (no pun intended). I expect my children to come to me for help when they are overwhelmed. Are you willing to humble yourself before your heavenly Father for help?

Isaiah 30:18 (AMP): "And therefore the Lord waits, longing to be gracious to you; and therefore He lifts Himself up, that He may have mercy on you and show loving-kindness to you. For the Lord is a God of justice. Blessed are those who wait for Him, who expect and long for Him, for His mercy, His victory, His favor, His love, His peace, His joy and His matchless, unbroken companionship." I believe the Lord longs for us to come to "the end of our rope," throw up our hands, raise the white flag and ask for His companionship. God expects a lot from us, so we must be willing to work with Him in all areas of our lives. Jesus will stick with you through it all! If you seek Him, read His Word and do your part, you'll be stronger than with any meal plan, behavioral video or hypnosis scheme that the world has to offer.

God gave us strengths and weaknesses. I don't particularly care for the weakness He decided to give to me—food! What was He thinking? I'm *surrounded* by food! It's everywhere I turn. I'm constantly bombarded with delicious stimuli. I have to go shop for the stuff, cook it, and clean all the stupid dishes it is placed on! Satan knows my weakness too. He entices me and trips me up when I try to have self-control. However, I've decided to fight back and take responsibility for my life. You can too!

I laced up my sneakers, covered my ears with my walkman, filled my heart and spirit with confidence, prayer and hope, and started walking. Walking is free and easy. And it works! About four years ago, we invested in a good treadmill so that my walking workout was not canceled due to darkness, weather conditions or safety concerns.

I'm sure many of you are thinking that you don't have the money or the space for a treadmill. Excuses! You have money to go out to eat, buy make-up and new clothes. For a few months, save your money so you can buy a treadmill. I put ours in the corner of our dark basement. I placed some bright posters on the cinder-block walls. My husband purchased a tiny, cheap television with a built-in VCR. I taped my favorite TV show and told myself that I could not watch it unless I was simultaneously walking on that treadmill! Quit making excuses! The time will fly because you're watching something that you really enjoy.

Now, let me tell you where I found the time. After I gave birth to our second child, I asked my husband, Rob, and myself a life-altering question. Do we want to have a neat and orderly home at all times, or would we prefer having me fit into my old jeans? Both of us chose me in my old jeans. I knew that I could not have both, because working out takes a chunk of time every day. I decided to let the housework slide a little so I could devote more time to me and my project. *You* are more important than the four walls surrounding you! I need to repeat that. *You* are more important than your house and the cleaning schedule!

I am a teacher, but please know that I do not have a degree in Fitness/Nutrition. I can only share some tips that have worked for me. Besides walking on the treadmill at least three times a week, I also lift handweights. I have two sets of weights—5 lb. and 10 lb. dumbbells. During a library visit with my children, I threw a few books about weight training in my bag. I learned a lot about burning fat and reshaping my body by lifting weights. I quickly saw results. Listening to good, fast music or watching a favorite show made the time pass quickly!

Did you know that when you have more muscle you can eat more? This is why your husband can get away with eating more than you do, yet not gain weight. Don't you just hate that!! I also highly recommend any of Denise Austin's "Hit the Spot" videos. They are 10-minute workouts that are tough but awesome. I exercise to her videos a few times a week.

I think the main thing is to vary your workouts. Do a workout tape one day; walk outside and work on stomach crunches the next time you work out. And be patient with yourself. Do 10 minutes a day for one week and then try 15 minutes of workout the next week. Increase your time, until you can work out for about one hour at least three or four times a week. And drink lots of water all day long. Many times we think we're hungry when we're just thirsty. Your skin will improve too!

Would you agree with me that God put us together in quite an amazing way? Think about it: He gave us tears to cry to help release the sadness in our hearts. He gave us antibodies to fight harmful germs that attack our bodies. We're designed with beautiful breasts that produce the "perfect food" for our babies. Do you know that He also gave you something to help you with the stress in your life? This "something" is already built into you. There are no pills, drinks or programs involved. When we exercise, our body releases chemicals called "endorphins."

Scientists have found that endorphins affect our brains and moods in a positive way. When you work out, it gives you a "natural high." This is why people who become regular exercisers tend to continue to exercise for the rest of their lives. They *like* the feeling they get! Do you think that this could be why God put them there? Should this not encourage us to continue doing this activity that is so beneficial to our bodies and also reduces the stress we feel every day?

Does God completely understand what stress is like for us? Jesus was a man—God made flesh. Can we even comprehend His "to do" list while He was here among us? I believe His handmade, dusty sandals saw a lot of walking miles. He has always been an example, hasn't He?

Prayer of the Day

Dear Father,

I need Your help. I desire balance in my life. I don't want to worry and obsess over food or my body. I have to learn to live with food without it controlling me. I want to enjoy food, but not lean on it. Help me to love myself. I want to be healthy and strong. I realize that to succeed in this weight project I must have discipline. I know that I am Your child and that Your children need discipline to be useful members of Your family. Lord, You know I have a lot to do today, but help me to relax and make time for myself. Help me to trust and call on You when I feel weak or tempted. I admit, I want to live a life with very little suffering and pain. This dieting and exercise plan are hard. Be with me. Comfort me. You offer companionship. I wholeheartedly accept it. I want my attitude to be different this time. I'll try my best to be patient, work hard, and not quit! Please help me, Lord, to turn this burden into a blessing. Amen.

Early Childhood Tip

The tip today is to do and live out the advice you just read. If you work out faithfully, you'll be setting a wonderful example for your children. Young children imitate us all the time. Children are watching us closely. They quickly learn what is important to us by how we spend our time. Even if your children are older, begin working out today.

Children that have parents who are voracious readers tend to love books themselves. Offspring of thespians many times "break a leg" in the theater. Does this guarantee that if you work out you'll have children that will grow up and work out? No. There are no guarantees. But your chances, I think, are very good. Your children will see that you have made exercise a part of your life. They will, in turn, incorporate it naturally into their lives.

My children have always seen me and my husband working out. When they were little, I would barricade the den and place them on a soft blanket with some toys. Next, I would roll out a towel, grab my weights and turn on good music to listen to while I worked out. I demonstrated, by example, that exercise was a valuable part of my day. The incredible added bonuses were: within a few short weeks of exercising, I had more energy (which I needed to chase my toddlers), had decreased my stress (due to those wonderful "endorphins") and felt better about my body!

With all the media pressure on young teenage girls today to be thin, I think that we, as moms, need to do everything we can to show balance to our young daughters. Satan must be thrilled with the stats on the number of teenage girls now suffering with bulimia and anorexia. I want to show my daughters (I have two beautiful girls) that you can eat well, but you must balance it with exercise. My girls are proud of me and often compliment me. That feels good! My daughter Brandy and I just finished a 10K race together!

There are some things that you cannot change. This is something you *can* change. You'll be amazed at what your body can do! You can be the best possible *you*. Get started! You are stronger than you think you are! America's self-proclaimed "court jester of health," Richard Simmons, says it best in his book *Richard Simmons Never Gives Up*: "I have blamed many people and many things for my fat, but I must admit I am to blame. I hold the fork."[*]

---

[*] Richard Simmons, *Richard Simmons Never Gives Up* (New York, NY: Warner Books, Inc.,1993), p. 341.

Chapter 16

Being Thankful

16

Thankful Hearts

Thank You, Lord, for the opportunity to sew all of these name tags onto my son's sweaters and jackets today.
My son is blessed to have more than one garment.

Thank You, Lord, for the parking space at the edge of the parking lot.
I have healthy, strong legs to get me to the door.

Thank You, Lord, that first thing this morning I had to be on hold (for ten minutes) waiting to schedule an appointment with my pediatrician.
My baby will be feeling better tonight.

Thank You, Lord, for that phone bill this month.
I could talk to my friend so very far away.

Thank You, Lord, for that sink with dirty dishes.
I had the chance to share another great meal with my family.

Thank You, Lord, for that noise (music) coming from my teen's room.
She is home—not a runaway.

Thank You, Lord, for that messy car in the garage. It needs a long bath.
I don't have to wait in the cold rain for a bus.

Thank You, Lord, that someone keeps sitting in my favorite seat at church every Sunday.
More people are coming to hear Your Word.

Thank You, Lord, for this messy bed that I must make once again.
   I didn't have to sleep on a dirty mat.

Thank You, Lord, for my husband arriving home late again.
   He has a good job, and he works hard at what he does.

Thank You, Lord, for the lost library book for which I've been searching the last two days.
   I live in an amazing country that allows me to check out any book I want.

Thank You, Lord, for my wait in the parking lot while my daughter finished her swimming lesson.
   I had time to listen to my favorite Christian music tape.

Thank You, Lord, for this list of names in my hand. My children are going to quite a few birthday parties this month and I must buy all of these kids a birthday present.
   My children are blessed with many wonderful friends.

Thank You, Lord, that one child needs a white sock for an art project tomorrow, another child needs a silly hat on Tuesday, and yet another child needs cupcakes for the bake sale and something that starts with the letter s today.
   My children are blessed with teachers that plan such fun-filled extra activities.

Thank You, Lord, for making me feel so yucky when I gossiped, lied, and became offended today.
   You love me so much that You want me to grow up spiritually. I'm glad You prune me, even though it hurts.

Thank You, Lord, for that ugly, tattered baby blanket my nine-year-old put in the laundry basket today. She checked on its condition many times during the laundering process. The blanket ("mass of threads" is more like it) must go into a special mesh bag. What concern over that stupid old thing!
   Someday I'll be grateful if she cares for me as tenderly, when I'm old, tattered and torn.

Thank You, Lord, for the report card that said my daughter is doing well academically, but tends to be too chatty and social.
> Praise God! I'm confident that as an adult she'll be chatty too—chatting to everyone about Jesus, her Lord and Savior. God puts us together for a very special purpose and reason. Love your kids the way they are.

Thank You, Lord, that my husband and I had to break our plans for a romantic, anniversary getaway from the kids.
> We can reschedule our plans. Unfortunately, plans do become broken. Fortunately, my children have not had their hearts broken over divorce.

Scripture to meditate on today:

1 Thessalonians 5:16–18
Be joyful always; pray continually; give thanks in all circumstances, for this is God's will for you in Christ Jesus.

Prayer of the Day

Heavenly Father,
Thank You for all of the blessings in my life. Help me to praise You all day long. When will I learn that grumbling and complaining erodes my faith and ruins my testimony? Help me to see the good, not the bad; the light, not the dark; the problem solver, not the problem. Help me to be flexible, patient, slow-to-anger, loving and kind. Remind me that I have the power to change my thinking from negative to positive. The flesh is weak, but Your Holy Spirit is inside of me, helping me go from mentally weak to mentally tough. I crave a better attitude. It is my choice today. I can have a bad attitude or a great one. I'm going to say it and believe it: I am the undefeatable child of God! I can do all things through Christ who strengthens me. When I have a disappointment today, let me see what I *have* and not what I have *not*.

Early Childhood Tip

I wish I knew who said this first, but I don't. However, it has become my motto, and I hope it will become yours also.

> Let my heart be broken
> By the things that break
> The heart of God.

Let me share an idea with you that will promote thankful hearts within your children and you. Franklin Graham (Billy Graham's son) heads a ministry called Samaritan's Purse. Millions of children have been touched by this ministry through "Operation Christmas Child." Every November, families, church groups and individuals reach out to needy children all over the world by sending shoeboxes filled with small gifts and the Good News of Jesus Christ (appropriately translated).

Simply contact Samaritan's Purse. They will send you a heart-warming video to show to your children, along with all the information you need to prepare and ship your boxes.

My children truly enjoyed doing this activity. They wrote a personal note to the children and included photos of themselves. They stuffed their boxes with chalk, crayons, coloring books, a doll, a hairbrush, bracelets, a jump rope, and lots of gum and hard candy. The entire project costs about $30.00. Everyone will leave this project with a thankful heart: thankful for the home and family we are blessed with—thankful for the chance to do something (a little something) for others in the name of Jesus Christ—thankful that even little hearts can share the good news and make another child happy.

Samaritan's Purse
International Headquarters
P.O. Box 3000,
Boone, NC 28607

Phone: (828) 262-1980
Fax: (828) 262-1796
Website: www.samaritanspurse.org

Franklin Graham, President

"All we have comes from God and we give it out of His hand."—1 Chronicles 29:14b, Dutch Paraphrase.

Chapter 17

Materialism

17

Do You Fall for the Mall?

I REMEMBER those "cabin fever" days when my two daughters were very young and I was pregnant with our third child. I would pack a few snacks and juice cups in my old, beat-up diaper bag and head for the mall. By the time I was dressed, had the kids in their snowsuits and had packed all of our "survival stuff," I felt almost too exhausted to go. (I know you are smiling right now. You know exactly what I'm talking about.)

The green plants and soothing water fountains in the mall were a welcome sight compared to the bleak winter day outside. My purse was usually light on cash. (Living on one salary can be tough.) But, I always had enough money for a yummy lunch for us. I saw so many nice clothes (my weakness) that I would have loved to try on. The children enjoyed looking in the big windows, tossing coins in the beautiful fountain, and watching all the people.

After the mall, we would return to our apartment and I would put the girls down for their afternoon nap. I would tiptoe out of their room with my picture books in hand and close the door quietly. That is *such* a delicious moment, isn't it? You won't be able to accomplish half of the "to do" list in your head, but at that moment—that special moment—you can sigh and actually pretend that you might be productive for a few hours. But, do you know what? On those mall days I sometimes felt dissatisfied upon returning home. I felt like I was missing out. I was dissatisfied with my clothes, the children's clothing, and my apartment. What had changed in just a few short hours? Satan is so subtle. While at the mall, I found that I was comparing myself to others. I had envied the ladies at the checkout counters with lovely new clothes draped over their arms. My kids were dressed nicely in their hand-me-down clothes, but they weren't wearing the Gap look. Usually, I don't care about stuff like that; I knew that my decision to be a full-time mother meant sacrifice with a capital *S*. Why was I caring about this now? Why the dissatisfaction?

Whenever we go to the mall, turn on the television, or dive into the circulars of our newspapers, we are being manipulated. Our feelings are being manipulated. The media and the companies that produce products or provide services are attempting to control us (what we buy, wear, drive, eat) or our circumstances (how we dress, where we eat, where we go for entertainment) to their advantage. Some use unfair and deceptive means. Are we playing right into their hands by letting them influence us so much? The men and women who own the corporations, market the products or create the ads, have an overblown, exaggerated view of the value of their product or services. They are experts at making us feel like we'll be left out if we don't buy their product. This plays on our feeling of wanting to "belong." They inform us that we should "indulge ourselves." We are worth it! This plays on our feelings of ego—me, ME, ME!

Satan's desire is for us to be dissatisfied and always longing for more. He knows that the more things we get, the more things we will want. If we have our minds on money and acquiring more stuff, we won't have our minds on the Lord. We won't be satisfied with our lives. We will lose our peace. (I lost *my* peace on those mall days.)

Look at Lot's life in the Old Testament. In Genesis 13:10–13 it talks about how Lot was greedy and always wanting the best. He blended in with the secular, materialistic society. Lot stopped making choices in God's direction and it led to his destruction: His life fell apart.

Money and things can ensnare us. People today have so many things. It takes time to keep all of those things working, cleaned and organized. It takes time away from our families and our fellowship with God. Do we need to downsize? But wait—there is a sale this weekend! Did you ever notice that there is one *every* weekend? The mall will open early and close late for us. They'll give us a free gift and we can sign up for more credit. Are you going to be there when the doors open? Lot will be there. He'll be the first one in line.

My younger daughter, Brandy, was really excited about studying Ancient Egypt. Her grandmother bought a few books for her about the ancient ruins. It's amazing what we have learned and continue to learn about this society. Everyone knows that the Egyptians were intelligent, were obsessed with preparation (mummification) for the afterlife, and revered felines. Now I've been trying to imagine what archaeologists might conclude about our society thousands of years from now . . .

"Loray, come over here!" Sarina shouted. Loray picked up the sparkly piece of glass in her hand, brushed it gently with her brush, and then turned and walked quickly towards her co-worker.

"What did you find?" Loray asked, as she peered over Sarina's shoulder. Sarina was looking out over an extensive pit. Men and women were working in the area below. Some were using sophisticated tools, such as electronic deep-earth scanners, and others were using hand-tools to gingerly unearth items found in the dirt.

"I think we've identified it. This site was a twentieth-century church. You know—a place where they worshiped their god," Sarina explained.

Loray looked puzzled. "Are you sure?" she asked. "I thought that you and Dr. Donovan were still unsure of the function of this large structure."

"Just look at the amount of land used to hold their form of transportation. The worshipers came in droves. I think they called these . . . parking lots," Sarina said. "Come over here to the layout we have of this site," she added with excitement, as she guided Loray to a table heavy with computers and ancient books. "We know this was a very important place. It is the largest ruin in a 30-mile radius. The building was made of marble and glass, and could hold many people at one time. They must have worshiped for long time-periods, because Chip's group found lots of food-container remnants. We think they must have dressed nicely to honor this god, for the crew yesterday found clothing scraps of the finest materials. Oh, oh, I even found evidence of a fountain in the center of the site today,"

Sarina continued, while twisting her hair into a ponytail. "Big screens were discovered on the northern end of the site. We are assuming that they were used to show pictures about their god, perhaps to instruct them on how to live in a holy way, or maybe to show the followers ways to spread the news about their religion."

"Interesting," Loray nodded, fascinated.

"We're still unsure, Loray, but I feel it has to be a church. Look at the size of the structure. Certainly, from all the research I've done, I can only conclude that this is where this culture worshiped. They made it big enough," Sarina said.

"And comfortable, too!" Loray added. "This is exciting," she agreed, placing her hands into her pockets. Her hand hit the piece of stained glass. She brought it out and placed it in her palm.

Sarina noticed and said, "Hey, I'm sorry. I've been so wrapped up in my find that I didn't even ask you about how your dig has been going over there." She pointed in the direction that Loray had come from earlier.

Loray's dig was very small compared to Sarina's assignment, but she was enjoying the work.

"Do you know what that small building you uncovered a few days ago was used for?" asked the ever-inquisitive Sarina.

"Well, so far it looks like it was just a small, ordinary building," Loray reported, as the young women turned and headed towards Loray's site. "It had crude, wooden seating inside. We found just a few golden bowls. I believe that this building probably had no real significance in the community. However, we'll keep digging." She smiled and held out her palm. "This piece of pretty glass is sort of interesting. I think I'll drive back later to the C.I.S. [Computer Information System—in the 20th century people called them "libraries"] and research this glass."

"Okay. Well, like you said, Loray, this dig was basically a shack. Don't waste too much time at the C.I.S. I'm going to talk to Dr. Donovan about having you moved over to my site. I could use you over here, on the important stuff," Sarina remarked, slapping Loray lightly on her back. Sarina left and her friend stared out over her little patch of earth.

Loray stepped to the edge of the smaller dig. Carefully, she stepped into the machine that would lower her slowly into the dark pit. When the shaky platform she was standing on reached the bottom of the excavation, she carefully stepped out onto the cool, brown earth. She never realized that a piece of paper, buried lightly in the rich dirt, was now stuck to the bottom of her boot. The small piece of wrinkled paper was a page from a hymnal. All one could make out on the yellowed artifact were the words "Amazing Grace," and a few musical notes. Loray never even noticed.

Matthew 6:24
No one can serve two masters. Either he will hate the one and love the other, or he will be devoted to the one and despise the other. You can not serve both God and Money.

To study Lot's life, look at:
Genesis 11:27–14:24 and 19:1–38
Luke 17:28–33
2 Peter 2:7–8

Prayer of the Day

Dear Lord,
You are a loving Father. You have blessed us in many ways. Help us to be satisfied with the things we have. You know the waywardness of our hearts and our minds. Help us to resist the temptations around us. Instead of desiring more clothes, shoes, and other possessions, help us to desire more of You. Forgive us for losing our way and putting material things ahead of spiritual matters. Be patient with us, Lord, as we strive for balance. Give us wisdom to see the way the world and Satan manipulate us, to keep us from having the peace that comes from trusting You. Amen.

Early Childhood Tip

This idea will help you when you go shopping with your little ones. It works!— if you use it consistently. Your children will learn quickly and you will avoid temper tantrums at the mall.

When I went shopping with my youngsters we had "looking days" and "buying days." Before you leave for the store, tell your children that today is a "looking day." Explain that they can look and touch (if non-breakable) the things at the store, but that you will not be buying any toys today. When you get to the store, make a mental note of the things they really loved. Compliment them on how well they are doing. "I like the way you held that bunny and then placed it back on the shelf." "Good job—maybe we could get that on a buying day!"

Stick to the plan. Do not buy them toys on "looking days." You might want to do what I did and give them small rewards for being a good listener. A piece of candy, some ice cream, a ride on those little rides found outside the store, or extra time at the playground are great ideas. Never buy them an expensive or big item on "looking days." This way your child will learn quickly that you mean what you say. Be consistent!

Once in a while, have a "buying day." Let your child pick something to buy that day. Seriously, your children will become excellent shoppers! My children keep a record of the things they really like. When it is a "buying day"—they know what they really want to purchase and which store stocks it!

This plan works even with toddlers. Start implementing it from Day One. I also feel that it is important to tell your children that you saw many things today on your shopping trip that you would have enjoyed buying for yourself, but didn't. This teaches, by example, that you have self-control. We need to show our children that we can't buy everything *we* see either! Remember, little eyes are watching you. Your children will grow to appreciate those "buying days"! Believe me!

Chapter 18

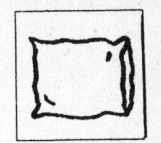

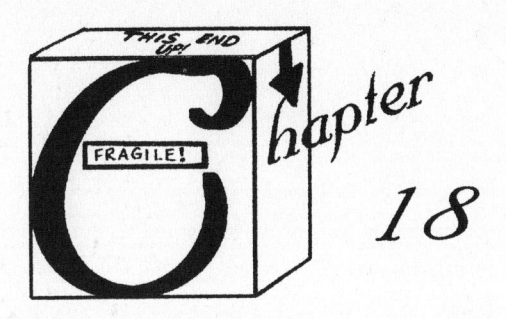

Sin

18

Moving

HOW do you spell stress? I spell it M-O-V-I-N-G. Moving is hard in every way. It's hard on your wallet, marriage, furniture, nerves, and your children. We moved last July—and yes, it was one of the hottest days of the summer. Once in our new place, my husband, Rob, and I tried to unpack a few things to entertain the children while we unpacked the rest of our lives. Our son, Hunter, then age six, seemed quite content to play on the computer while his sisters tried to organize their new room. All was well until the end of the day, when Rob called me into our bedroom.

"I think Hunter put some files in the trash can," Rob said, looking at the computer monitor. His face told me he was worried.

"What?" I yelled. "Are you sure?"

Most of you know this already, but for those of you who are resisting the computer, I'll give you the picture: When you drag a file into the trash-can symbol, the computer will ask you if you are sure you want to delete the file. If you push "yes," then the file gets erased. You *can't* get it back! Usually Hunter works on the computer closely supervised, but with the commotion of moving he was alone and could have easily deleted some important files.

Fortunately, the files were not erased, only moved. Whew! Needless to say, I had a little talk with Hunter the next day. I explained the importance of the little trash-can symbol on our computer screen.

Later in the week, while unpacking my china, my mind returned to the trash-can episode with Hunter. I was really concerned about those files. I knew some of those files were favorites, and the children would have been sad to lose them. Once deleted, they are gone.

Why can't we, I mused, regularly give our sins to God and let Him place them in *His* trash can? He will forget about them. Gone! Erased! Unretrievable! I thought of my life as a computer screen. (You should know by now that when I start examining MY LIFE, that's when I'm hoping that you, too, are examining YOUR LIFE. Hmmmm. Don't let me go through this alone.)

You should see my lovely, serene computer screen background! (Okay, again for those of you out there that are computer challenged, the background picture comes on when you turn the computer on.) My computer background looks like a large postcard from Colorado. The majestic mountains and the clear blue sky looks so real you can almost smell the pines. There is a crystal-clear lake with the sunlight dancing on top of it. All right, now let's get *real* and use the mouse to click to see what is really behind my INNER screen. I have quite a few "saved" files. Why do I save this stuff—past sins, past offenses, horrible mistakes? Why can't I just drag them down to the trash can where they clearly belong and forget them? Why don't I confess them and let my Savior place them in God's trash can? Instead, I keep them on the screen, but move them around. Of course, I cleverly avoid double-clicking on them most of the time. A double click would open them up and flood my screen with guilt. Right? But do I truly understand how this unconfessed sin damages my fellowship with my Lord and Savior?

God's compassion is greater than any sin in your life. In the Bible, He promises forgiveness. God looks at who we are today and what we will become. Nobody is beyond redemption. Nobody is so sinful that he or she can't become clean through the blood of Jesus Christ.

We walk around with baggage—"saved files." Oftentimes, we beat ourselves up with these saved mistakes. That's so wrong! Let's become radically obedient, and when we slip and fall back into sinful patterns let's quickly give the file to God, who will put it in His trash can and delete it forever. When a file (our sin) goes into the trash can, it cannot be retrieved. God will forget all of your sins and so should we.

If we let Him, He will format new programs into our minds and hearts—through His Word and His Spirit. It is never too late to get "on line" with God.

Prayer of the Day

Dear Heavenly Father,

Today I bring to You the unconfessed sins that I have in my heart. I get discouraged by how easy it is for me to fall back into old patterns. I know that You hate my *sin* but love *me*. I need You, Jesus, to comfort me when I fall. These setbacks are difficult for me, because I want so much to mature in my walk with You. Your commands and laws are hard. Yet I know in my heart that they open the door to a cavern of rich blessings and spiritual liberation for me. Thank You for paying the price for my sins—all the sins I've already done and all the sins I will do. They are at the foot of the cross, each one bordered with Your life-changing blood.

Scripture to meditate on today:

Lamentations 3:21–23 (TLB)

Yet there is one ray of hope: his compassion never ends. It is only the Lord's mercies that have kept us from complete destruction. Great is his faithfulness; his lovingkindness begins afresh each day.

Isaiah 1:18

"Come now, let us reason together," says the Lord. "Though your sins are like scarlet, they shall be as white as snow; though they are red as crimson, they shall be like wool."

1 John 1:8–9

If we claim to be without sin, we deceive ourselves and the truth is not in us. If we confess our sins, he is faithful and just and will forgive us our sins and purify us from all unrighteousness.

John 8:34–36

Jesus replied, "I tell you the truth, everyone who sins is a slave to sin. Now a slave has no permanent place in the family, but a son belongs to it forever. So if the Son sets you free, you will be free indeed."

Romans 5:20–21(TLB)

The Ten Commandments were given so that all could see the extent of their failure to obey God's laws. But the more we see our sinfulness, the more we see God's abounding grace forgiving us. Before, sin ruled over all men and brought them to death, but now God's kindness rules instead, giving us right standing with God and resulting in eternal life through Jesus Christ our Lord.

Early Childhood Tip

I hope that you are blessed with a PC in your home. You'll need a computer, a few sheets of white paper, black crayons and a trash can for this activity.

Part 1: Talk to your children about the trash-can symbol on your computer screen. Explain how once files are placed into the trash can and deleted, they cannot be retrieved. Show them how this is also a demonstration of how we can give our sin to God and how He forgives us.

For discussion starters, ask: Why is it important for us to tell God about our sin and ask for forgiveness? (Discuss the effects of guilt.) Do you think God hates the sin? (Yes.) How does He feel about us? (He loves us very much.) What happens to real trash if we don't deal with it right way? (It smells, rots.) Is that like guilt and condemnation?—older children. Is it best to get rid of garbage right away?—smaller kids. How do you feel after you talk to God about your sin? (Clean again.) Do you think God wants us to carry around some smelly trash—our old sins—all the time? (Of course not.) He died so we could be free from that.

Adapt your questions and discussions to the age and spiritual maturity of your children.

Part 2: Give your children each a piece of white paper and a black crayon. Ask your children to write down a sin that they have done recently, maybe even today. For 3 and 4-year-olds, have them draw a picture. Here are some examples: I took something that wasn't mine. I was unkind to my sister. I was selfish and didn't share. I said something that wasn't true. You could say something like, "Is there anything that you did today or recently that broke God's heart, or made Him sad?" Then they should shade in (with the black crayon) the border of the paper. This should make the paper look dirty. Isn't sin dark and dirty?

Next, everyone should sit in a circle on the carpet. Place a trash can in the middle of the circle. On the side of the trash can, tape a piece of white paper with a picture of a cross. Tell your children that when you call their name out loud, they should crumple their paper in their hands and put it in the trash can (the cross). Tell them that they are confessing their sin and giving it to Jesus. Invite each child to return to his original spot on the carpet.

Tell everyone to hold out their hands. Ask them, "What is in your hands now?" They'll tell you that their hands are empty, which will give you the chance to illustrate how once sin is confessed and given to the Lord, it is gone. We don't have to feel guilty (bad) anymore, but we must try to honor God by not doing that sin again. Oh, I almost forgot—*you also* must write down a sin on a piece of paper and place it in the "cross" trash can. Let your children see you as a sinner, but a sinner who is moving toward a higher level of Christian maturity. Now, that's the only kind of moving I like!

Chapter 19

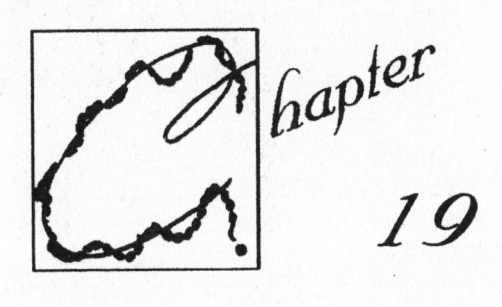

Irritations/Strength

19

Lookin' Forward to Bein' Shucked!

MOMS know that when you go out for dinner and you take the kids along with you, by the end of the meal you'll have visited the restroom of the restaurant at least twice, maybe more times. Oh, it's extra fun getting to the bathroom in record time when your kids are wearing their new "training pants." You may recall the days when you wanted the hostess to seat you near the window for the great view, or perhaps in a corner booth so you could steal a kiss from your husband while enjoying a sinfully chocolate dessert. Forget that! Now, you just pray that the hostess will seat you close enough to the bathroom so that your little one can only utter "I gotta go! I gotta go!" five or six times (max), before you hit the bathroom door running!

Last spring my husband, my parents, the children and I were dining at one of my favorite seafood restaurants, "Fisherman's Inn." (If you zip around the city of Baltimore, Maryland, head for the Chesapeake Bay, cross over on the beautiful suspension bridge near Annapolis—saluting to your right as you see the U.S. Naval Academy in the distance—and land on the "salty" Eastern Shore, then you'll run right into the "Fisherman's Inn.") On one of my many trips to the bathroom with our three children I couldn't help but notice the awesome display of dishes adorning the walls on the way to the restroom. They looked like antiques (they are), yet they were odd in that they were round and usually had six indentations. I finally realized I was looking at a collection of 300 oyster plates. Each of the little indentations was made to cup a delicious oyster.

On the way home in the car, I asked my husband if he knew

what caused oysters to make a pearl ... the pretty plates still on my mind. (My favorite plates were those decorated in pearls.) He told us that if an irritant (like a grain of sand) got inside an oyster's shell, the mantle, which is the outer part of the oyster's soft body, would secrete shell material around the irritant to protect itself from it. Eventually the shell material would build up and become a pearl. (He said it in much more technical, biology-teacher language, but I've condensed it for us.) I thought that was so interesting. An iridescent pearl is created all because of something that bothered a little oyster!

Do you have some things that are irritating you right now? Every day, and many times during each day, we have things that come against us, that definitely irritate us. How are we going to handle those irritations? Are we going to let them consume us and ruin our day or are we going to call on God, cooperate, and let Him make those irritants into a shiny pearl?

When the grain of sand gets into the oyster's shell, the mantle starts secreting the shell-building cells around the irritant—sort of like a barrier to protect the soft oyster. That makes me think of what Jesus does for us. When Satan pries into our lives (our shell) and gives us a temptation or an irritating situation, we can rely on the Lord to start protecting us and helping us to deal with that irritation. We have a choice as to our reaction. We can be led by the Holy Spirit, who will tell us to do one thing, or be led by our flesh, which will certainly want us to do the exact opposite.

After researching the oyster, I discovered that when the grain of sand encounters hard muscular tissue on the oyster, it interferes with the mantle's ability to completely cover the irritant and so the pearl ends up oddly formed. Pearls of this sort are called "baroque pearls." Are our hearts hard sometimes? Do we have opinions, grudges, and stubborn wills that interfere with the way God would have us handle those grains of sand that come into our lives? I don't know about you, but I'm sure that in my Christian "jewelry box" I must not have merely a *few* baroque pearls. No, I'm sure I've collected a whole baroque necklace, a baroque bracelet and matching baroque earrings by now! I've handled so many situations the wrong way, been guilty of letting Satan persuade me in the wrong direction.

Many times it is not even Satan, but just our own selfishness and pride; we just enjoy blaming things on him. We lose our peace. But God is using Satan's attacks and life's problems and inconveniences to build our character.

When will we learn to deal with these things not in our *own* strength but *God's*?

Have you felt pressed in from all sides? Well, so has the oyster. I also found out that the cute little starfish, one of my favorite beach-walk finds (until today), is the enemy of oysters and other mollusks like clams and mussels. The starfish attaches its strong arms to both the top and bottom of the oyster shell and tries to pull it apart. This can go on for a long period of time, until the weakened oyster finally gives up. The oyster's abductor muscle relaxes and the starfish pulls the oyster shells apart. It then squeezes some of its stomach into the shell opening. This, of course, causes the oyster distress and he opens his shell even more, and the starfish is ready and waiting to pour more of its stomach into the oyster and swallow it.

Temptations are waiting for us, pressing in around us, waiting for a weak spot in our shell. Once they come into our lives and we act on them, they can and will consume us. What determines whether the starfish will be able to open the oyster quickly or not? The strength of the oyster's abductor muscle varies with the condition and the size of the particular oyster. We worry about the condition of our yards, our homes, and our finances, but our eyes ought to be on the condition of our Christian walk. How strong is it? Jesus died to give us strength: are we taking advantage of this? Jesus died on the cross for you so you could live with Him in heaven, but He also died so you could have strength *now*.

> Isaiah 40:29 (NKJV)
> *He gives power to the faint; and to those that have no might he increases strength.*
>
> Philippians 4:13 (NKJV)
> *I can do all things through Christ who strengthens me.*
>
> Ephesians 6:10 (NKJV)
> *Finally, my brethren, be strong in the Lord and in the power of his might.*

Temptations are not going to go away. In the Bible, Jesus warned about two things over and over. Those two things are *Satan* and *money* (greed). I guess He felt they would be huge stumbling blocks and so He left us many warnings about them. When I look at the problems in our world, I realize how wise Jesus was in warning us. The problems are still the same. But . . . hope is still alive. We know that Christ defeated Satan on the cross and that his time is short. Our suffering will result in pearls if we abide in Christ Jesus.

Romans 5:3
Not only so, but we also rejoice in our sufferings, because we know that suffering produces perseverance; perseverance, character; and character, hope. And hope does not disappoint us, because God has poured out his love into our hearts by the Holy Spirit, whom he has given us.

Most watermen will agree that the starfish is definitely an enemy. A starfish's power to regenerate missing arms and body parts is incredible. Before they understood this, frustrated watermen would catch the starfish in nets that they dragged on the bottom of the sea floor; then they would cut the starfish up into tiny pieces, thinking they were killing them, and toss the fragments back into the water. Unfortunately, they were making the situation worse, because the starfish could regenerate themselves!

Some starfish or sea stars can reform completely even from a tiny piece of tissue, such as the mouth! We must guard our hearts and minds against temptations—big ones and little ones. There have been temptations in my life that I tried to fight on my own. Oh, I confidently went to the starboard railing and tried to fight and kill the temptations by myself. I would cut them into little pieces: little pieces of excuses, little pieces of rationalizations and more. I threw them all overboard, looked back and watched them mix in with the wake of my own path. But I was as foolish as the watermen cutting up starfish. The temptations came back. I wasn't living a victorious life until I asked God to be my strength.

2 Corinthians 4:7–8
This all-surpassing power is from God and not from us. We are hard pressed on every side, but not crushed.

When the starfish is not busy eating his fill on the oyster bed, he has also been known to enter unattended fishing nets and help himself to the day's catch. Watermen in Maine are disgusted when they pull their lobster pots out of the cold Atlantic and find starfish munching on their lobster bait! Nasty!

Well... man has found one good use for the starfish. Sometimes large quantities of them are crushed and used as fertilizer. Hmmm. ... Those pesky starfish can make things grow? I like to look at all the things pressing in on me in that light, too. I don't like the inconveniences or the pressure from hassles and problems, but they do make me grow. What Satan meant for our harm and destruction, God will turn into a good thing.

Since I was reading and thinking about oysters so much, I sort of became hungry for oyster stew or something, so I decided to look through the many seafood cookbooks that my mother-in-law has given to me. I was surprised at how each cookbook warned about the improper handling of fresh oysters. They are really fragile!

The abductor muscle in the oyster begins to relax if you shake or handle the oyster too roughly or warm it above a certain temperature. This causes the oyster's valves to gap, the water inside is lost and the oyster soon dies. Moms, our children are fragile too. Use this time while they are preschoolers and at home with you to gently train them up in the ways of the Lord.

Talk to them about God and His Son, Jesus. Sing Bible songs with them and play Christian lullaby tapes in their rooms as they drift off to sleep. Take them to church. If you aren't happy with the one you belong to, find another one that you do enjoy. Pray with your kids and for them. Enroll them in vacation Bible school and volunteer your own services! A child patterns his life after the models before him! Keep your priorities straight.

Teach your children at an early age about Satan. They understand a loving God, and they will also understand about a fallen angel. Good and bad is easy for them. Warn them that Satan will try to convince them to do things that God would not want them to do. How comforting for them to know that God is on their side, and able to help them make the right choices when they pray and ask for His help. This empowers your children! I see it happening with my own. Build strong spiritual muscles now to help before the world gets them, shakes them up, turns up the temperature and handles them roughly!

This world is not our home. Heaven is our home. You know what—we should be anxious to be shucked! How awesome to get rid of this shell of a body and meet our Lord and Savior. We'll hand Him our pitiful earthly jewelry boxes filled with all those baroque pearls and He'll exchange them for the faultless ones . . . our eyes won't be able to take in all the perfect pearls that He wants to give us, their luster and translucence unimaginable!

Prayer of the Day

Heavenly Father,

I should never feel weak; not when I can open my Bible and be reassured of the strength I have in You. Over and over You assert that I don't have to handle life by myself. You desire to be my strength. Satan comes against me and my own wishy-washy feelings interfere with the way that I should handle the irritants in my life. I'm tired; I'm exhausted. I know I love You, Lord. And I know that You want me to have peace and joy. You paid a high price for that. Help me die to the things that are blocking my way. Help me to change. Help me to strengthen my spiritual muscles. Things certainly get lopsided when my stubbornness gets in the way. Thanks for loving me even if I am lopsided, Lord. My many "mommy" responsibilities are pressing on my fragile shell right now, but I won't run and I won't give in. You are my hope. Amen.

Early Childhood Tips

Here are some helpful family tips that I've used when we've been blessed with a trip to the seashore.

• Safety/Peace of Mind Tips •

- When your children are very young and don't care about making a fashion statement, dress them all in the same brightly colored bathing suits. This way you'll be able to find them very easily when you look into the crowd at the water's edge. After sunset, when you treat yourselves to a night of junk-food eating on the boardwalk, dress your kids in identically colored sweatshirts or T-shirts for easy spotting.

• Prepare a car trip bag to entertain your gang on the road. Fill it with library books about pelicans, beaches of the world, waves, ocean life, and unusual fish. Include some snacks that you don't usually purchase, plain paper for drawing and writing, and photo albums filled with photos of past seaside vacations. If you want to hear tons of giggles in the car, slip in some old photos of you and your husband when you two were young and at the beach.

• So that your children can find you and your "stuff" on the beach, tie a neon-bright lightweight scarf to your beach umbrella. The refreshing sea breeze will keep the scarf (or thick ribbon) flapping in the breeze and be a easy marker for your children when they get disoriented and see 15 umbrellas that are exactly the same color. If you don't own or aren't renting an umbrella, tie the bright ribbon to your beach chair.

Your trip to the beach should be fun and relaxing. However, the teacher in me wants to convince you to learn a few facts before your vacation so that you will not only impress your kids with your "beach knowledge" but will also make the trip as educational as possible.

Don't roll your eyes and say that you won't be able to learn these facts or be able to remember them. Don't you remember your high school and college days? We memorized chemical tables, all of the U.S. Presidents, the countries of Eastern Europe and lots of other charts, tables, etc. Seriously, have we really used most of those memorized facts? No. What we really needed to memorize was a list of edible recipes you can make in less than five minutes, the top-secret list of blue jean manufactures in the free world that produce reinforced knees in their jeans, and a multitude of interesting facts to tell your little kids at the seashore when they say, "Mommy, what's this?"

Now get crackin', study and learn the facts below and watch their eyes bug out in amazement that you know so many coooool things! I tried to pick items that you might commonly see on a beach walk or while visiting a barrier island. I'm writing this in a style as if I were speaking to a young child.

- **Seaweeds** - Plants that live in the ocean are called seaweeds. Most seaweeds are a kind of algae. They need the sunshine to make their food. A long time ago, the Romans (this was around the time Jesus lived) would put seaweed on a burn or skin rash. Some sailors, long ago, would eat some types of seaweed if they had an upset tummy. Right now, there are factories that are using ground-up seaweed to make ice cream, candy, and cake icings. When we see "carrageenin" on a food label, then we'll know it has seaweed in it!

- **Horseshoe crabs** - The horseshoe crab looks like a crab, but he is not a normal crab. He moves like a crab and has a hard shell like a crab, but he has some unique features. When you turn him over, he looks like a horseshoe, but with a long tail. Sometimes a strong wave tips him over and he lands upside down on the beach. That is when he gets busy using his long, strong tail to flip himself over. When the American Indians made their spears they would use the tails of horseshoe crabs for the tips.

- **Jellyfish** - How do you think they got their name? They are soft and wiggly like jelly. One kind of jellyfish is a sea nettle. Their bodies look like a clear upside-down bowl or an umbrella. When they are floating in the water, they have long thin arms that look like spaghetti, but are called tentacles. The spaghetti arms of most jellyfish are dangerous, because if they rub against you when you are swimming in the water, they will sting you. It feels like a bee sting. They sting fish and the poison goes into the fish and stuns it. Then the jellyfish pulls the fish up to his mouth and has fish for lunch. Never touch a jellyfish.

- **Seagulls** - There are around 8,000 different kinds of birds in the world. Gulls are a shorebird. They live around the shores of the oceans. Seagulls are very coordinated with their wings. They glide and soar in the wind. Seagulls like to carry mussels (explain the difference between *muscle* and *mussel*) up into the air and drop them on the rocks to break open the shell and then eat the animal inside. They are scavengers—that means they are the beach "clean-up crew" and eat the stuff that people leave behind.

- **Starfish and oysters** - I probably have already told you more than you ever wanted to know about these two critters.

Chapter 20

Reward

20

Mittens

MY TOE was tapping. My arms were definitely crossed. My three children looked up at me and knew the "mommy explosion" was coming and soon! The four of us were crammed into our tiny "mud room" by our back door. It was a morning in December. Book bags, coats, and sneakers carpeted the floor. (Why can't I have one of those organized and well-decorated mud rooms like I see in the magazines? Tidy. Decorator perfect. Stop comparing, Liz, this is real life. You are off the track. Get back to yelling at your three little darlings.)

"What do you mean you've lost your mittens again?" I yelled. "We'll look in the lost and found," stammered Brielle, my fourth grader. "I have one mitten, Mom, and I think the other one is in my locker at school," Brandy (age 9) added quickly. Hunter, my six-year-old, just looked up at me and shrugged his shoulders. "Okay, listen up," I said, exasperated. "Today, I am going to buy a new pair of mittens for each of you. The person who still has those very same mittens on the first day of spring—will win a prize." They seemed excited about this new idea. I gave them each a quick kiss and sent them out the door to walk to school. Why did you say that? I asked myself. And what prizes are you going to give them? What if one of them loses in the contest? They weren't toddlers anymore, but I knew I had to try to do something to teach them responsibility for their things.

It was amazing. It was a miracle. My three kids treated their new mittens like new pets. I didn't find mittens in the shoe closet, nor did I find them under the kitchen table. No. They were together, housed neatly in book bags. I overheard the girls whispering guesses about what the "spring prize" might be.

In February, right around Valentine's Day, they wanted to know how many days until spring. (Was this all I had to do? I should have done it years ago. The cash-register receipt tape depicting past mitten, scarve and hat purchases seemed long enough to swirl around my neck and wrap around my feet!)

We all enjoy receiving rewards, don't we? Matthew 16:27 says, "For the Son of Man is going to come in his Father's glory with his angels, and then he will reward each person according to what he has done." 2 Chronicles 15:7 states: "But as for you, be strong and do not give up, for your work will be rewarded." These verses convict and comfort me. God will look at our lives and examine how we dealt with opportunities He provided. He has given us gifts (yes, you have one or more—probably plenty) and time. Are we spending our gifts and time on things that will last? Things that have eternal value? I believe these verses are there not to make us feel guilty but to warn us—a sign to be careful.

We are all on a journey. We live in a very secular world. We have to work, pay bills, clean our homes and do a variety of other things. But we must not let our enemy, Satan, steal all of our time. He doesn't want us to spend any time with God, or in doing God's work. Satan knows that the more we abide in Jesus and balance our lives with prayer, worship and service, the more joy and peace we'll have in our lives. How true! And heaven lies ahead! Can you imagine how wonderful it'll be? The Bible gives us some information, but I still can't comprehend how great it will be for believers.

God's salvation is a free gift. Jesus died on the cross to obtain it for us. We cannot do some "good work" to get into heaven. By accepting Jesus Christ as our Savior we become children of God. But, as you grow from a baby Christian (one recently born-again) into a spiritually mature Christian, you find yourself wanting to do more and more for Christ. You can't help it. Spiritual energy spills out of you. You fall in love with Jesus; you are so thankful for what He has done for you. You want others to have the peace and joy that you have found in the Lord.

The Bible tells us our reward is coming. The world may not see what you are doing; you may not get any credit now from anyone—but remember, God sees and knows your heart. He sees you when you cook that meal and take it to that sick neighbor. God smiles when you send that check in the mail to that favorite ministry of yours. He watches as you stay up late preparing that Sunday school lesson. Your reward is coming. Hang in there! Don't lose your mittens!!!

Prayer of the Day

Dear Heavenly Father,

Being in heaven with You is going to be reward enough. Help me to not give up. I feel so tired and overwhelmed. Help me to listen to Your call, Lord. Help me to find my gifts and to use my time wisely. Help me to handle all the stuff I need to do. I'm trying to be a good wife, mommy, daughter, sister, etc. . . . I want to have time for You, God. I know that my work for You is for eternity. Others may regard me as "different," but help me to be strong in character. Help me to be obedient and stand tall for You. Help me also to not compare myself with my other Christian brothers and sisters. Help me to remember we all have different gifts, and each one is important in the body of the church. God, I know You love me and have a plan for my life. I give up my life and ask You to use me. I know that You do not place worth and value upon what we *do* but who we *are* in You. Help me to be all You want me to be. In Jesus' precious name I pray. Amen.

Early Childhood Tip

When my children reached the second grade, I implemented a new rule. Everyone loses things—so each child was allowed one lost article (coat, hat, sweater, etc) per school year. But if they lost a second article they had to pay for half of the cost to replace it. (If they don't earn an allowance, then they can do small jobs around the house for you.) They will not enjoy using their own money to replace clothing. This works, believe me.

I also sew their names in everything! That surely helps.

Why not try the "mittens until spring" idea. The prize could be a dinner at their favorite restaurant; browsing, then choosing a favorite book at a bookstore; or renting two great movies and staying up waaaaayyyyy past their normal bedtime.

Chapter 21

Prayer

21

Praying on Holy Ground

THE LARGE cardboard box next to the front door was filled with the supplies I would need for the next day: new tubes of oil paints, linseed oil, a supply of new paintbrushes, sketch pads, old rags, and my old palette from college. "What was I thinking when I agreed to do an oil painting for the church?" I asked myself as I crumbled to the couch. I stared at the box and the large white canvas leaning against the wall. The canvas was so white, so big, so blank! I could feel the beads of perspiration on my brow, for I had only two days to complete this painting. My husband was planning on minding our seven-month-old for the weekend. Refusing to expose our baby to the harmful fumes, I planned on doing the painting at the church.

That evening I spent a lot of time in prayer. "Please give me a sign that this is going to work out" was the fervent prayer of a sleep-deprived art minor with six mediocre paintings under her belt. At this point in my spiritual journey I was just beginning to abide in the Lord, and was attending a women's Bible study for the first time in my life. Even today, when I think about what happened the next morning, it still gives me goose bumps!

I woke up early and gulped down some coffee. My churning stomach convinced me to skip breakfast. I kissed Rob and our baby girl, Brielle, placed my box of supplies under my arm, and reached for the huge canvas. I clumsily made my way out of the doorway and then almost dropped everything when I saw a white dove flying towards me. The bird landed right in front of me on the sun-splashed sidewalk.

The dove was plump and snow white. She wasn't frightened; instead she bravely hopped towards me and cocked her head from side to side. Her eyes seemed friendly and wise. She blocked my path and was in no hurry to move out of my way. In her mouth was a twig with five or six small green leaves attached to it. We looked at each other for what seemed like a long time (but in actuality was probably only a minute) before she flew away.

I stood there shocked. I knew that God had just graced me with a sign, a vision if you will, so that I could gather up the confidence to do this painting. I laughed out loud at God's timing, wisdom and sense of humor.

God knew about the sketches I had just completed the day before. It was no surprise to God that my painting was to have Noah standing at the ark's railing, arm extended, to provide a perch for the dove flying towards him. And yes, the dove in my sketch was white as snow and had an olive branch in his beak, just like in the ancient story. A sign for Noah . . . a sign for Elizabeth.

I wish I could say that I get signs like these all the time but, unfortunately, that is not the case. I have to admit that even though my age was twenty-eight, I was truly a "baby Christian" when this happened. I guess God knew I needed that vision to encourage me in my Christian walk. Now, after all these years, He expects me to trust a little bit more.

In the twenty-first century we are very concerned about getting things done, yet we desire some sense of peace in our lives. We feel rushed, over-worked and stressed out! The answer to this problem is found in the Bible. It's found in prayer. Prayer isn't for God; prayer is for *us*. Philippians 4:6–8 (TLB): "Don't worry about anything; instead, pray about everything; tell God your needs and don't forget to thank him for his answers. If you do this you will experience God's peace, which is far more wonderful than the human mind can understand. His peace will keep your thoughts and your hearts quiet and at rest as you trust in Christ Jesus."

The world tries to convince us that it has the answer for our emotional distress. Satan will entice us to drink or drug ourselves into a happier place. *Empty* peace! The secular world hopes we'll sign up for a new stress-buster workout, try out a new herb, or buy yet another magazine with its 177 ways to get the stress out of our lives! *Artificial* peace! If only we would humble ourselves and spend our time on our knees in prayer to the Father who made us and loves us with an everlasting love! Why are we looking to the world to "de-stress" us? Who made us? Prayer lets us release our stress by giving our burdens, our anger, our disappointments and our still unfulfilled dreams, to a Father who loves us more than we can ever comprehend.

Finding the best time to pray is tricky, but well worth it. It must be a priority. I'm probably just like you in that I like it when God answers my prayer quickly; however, I'm not too fond of the times when He says no, closes doors on MY plans, or when He is silent and nothing seems to be happening.

In Leith Anderson's book *Praying to the God You Can Trust*, he writes, "God often says no because He has something better planned for those He loves. Our hearts can well up with thankfulness to God that He knows what is better and more important."* Anderson spoke to my heart when he wrote: "He [God] teaches us that today's disappointment will make sense tomorrow. In everything He acts with a higher priority on achieving our good than on simply granting our prayers."*

When will we learn to appreciate "no" and closed doors? Let's look expectantly for His open window. Sometimes we must wait for our prayers to be answered. We need to rest while we wait. Let's bask in the sun and salty wind like a seasoned first mate waiting for the captain to tell him the next course to set. And when will we be thankful for the "yes"—the answered prayer? Let's run to our Father and shower Him with words of thankfulness and praise for all that He has done and is doing.

There is a sweet story about President Abraham Lincoln that goes something like this: One day President Lincoln was attending to his official business, trying to work through his schedule crammed with appointments. An elderly woman asked to see him. He graciously consented, and escorted her into his office. He asked how he could be of service ... ever the public servant! She told him that

---

* Leith Anderson, *Praying to the God You Can Trust* (Minneapolis: Bethany House), pp. 132 and 126.

she did not come to ask him for anything. She went on to tell him that she had heard that he was fond of a certain kind of cookie, and she gave him a box full of them. The smell of freshly baked cookies filled the air and caused the president to smile. Tears welled up in his eyes as he realized that this dear woman had baked him some treats and taken the time to bring them to him. Lincoln let her know that she was the very first person who had ever come into his office asking and expecting nothing, but rather bringing a gift for him.

We could learn from this story of sincere thanksgiving. Do we always have a list of requests for God? Let's go to Him some days with just gratitude and praise . . . how fragrant . . . what a treat for our King!

I'm finding that I truly need prayer. Jesus set such a wonderful example by getting away alone and praying. He needed time with His Father. I need time with God; you, too, probably need more time with God! This is how we're put together. C. S. Lewis (one of my favorite authors) says it best: "God made us: invented us as a man invents an engine. A car is made to run on gasoline, and it would not run properly on anything else. Now God designed the human machine to run on Himself. He Himself is the fuel our spirits were designed to burn. . . . There is no other. That is why it is just no good asking God to make us happy in our own way without bothering about religion. God cannot give us a happiness and peace apart from Himself, because it is not there."* People try other ways, but can never be truly happy or at peace.

In 1 Thessalonians 5:17 you find, "Pray continually." It took me a while to really understand that verse. I used to be the kind of Christian that would pray and think about God on Sunday while at church. I would "fill up" my tank on Sunday. I would feel so strong and peaceful. Why wasn't I realizing that my tank was empty by Tuesday, or before? I'm much happier now that I make prayer a part of my day *every* day. I pray while I'm in the shower; I pray while doing the dishes. I have an awareness of the Lord's presence with me throughout the day, and I talk to Him continually.

At one point in my Christian walk I envied people who said they heard from God. Why didn't I hear from God? What was wrong

---

* C. S. Lewis, *Mere Christianity* (New York: Simon & Shuster, 1996), p. 54.

with me? Then I began to pray for wisdom. I asked God to give me a quiet spirit and ears to hear His voice. He did and I do. Oh boy, be careful what you pray! Sometimes His voice is loud and clear. He points out lots of things that I need to change. It is painful when He illuminates my weaknesses, but He is trustworthy. Along with His rebuke and chastisement you'll also hear the affirmation. God communicates back to us through our circumstances, through other people, and by a clear, quiet voice inside of us—the Holy Spirit.

Many of you who are reading this book are already enjoying a strong prayer life. But there may be some readers who suffer from a hollow prayer life. They may feel unsure of how to pray, or what to say. Still, they desire to build a richer prayer life. If I've just described you, start with simple prayers. Open up your heart and tell God exactly how you feel.

You may want to turn in the Bible to the book of Psalms. This wonderful collection of prayers and songs reflects humanity at its best, revealing deep emotions and fears. The psalms are comforting to read, especially if you have a Bible (like the Life Application Bible) that explains the scriptures. Remember, your style of prayer is personal and unique, just like your fingerprints and your voice. There is no formula or "right way" to do it. Be confident that God cares about you and has promised in the Bible to hear your prayers.

I think our church pulpits have in some ways failed to teach us the power and importance of prayer. We need to hear our spiritual leaders encouraging us to constantly turn our worries into prayers. When trials and problems come against us, are we trained to avoid analyzing the situation to death? Are we equipped to shun anger (towards God, others, or even ourselves) and prepared for a dependence on God through prayer? Are we reminded that God will carry us through trials and that they will benefit us in time? God's children need regular doses of Romans 8:28: "And we know that in all things God works for the good of those who love him, who have been called according to his purpose."

Prayer changes things. When you pray, you are making your prayer space "holy ground." On this parcel of holy ground you can boldly claim "stakes"—ground you have claimed as your own. This prayer space may include your personal needs, prayers for loved ones, requests for wisdom, prayers for God's Church and the unsaved. Each stake, each prayer, will be lifted high and heard by God. We must stop being wimpy, hand-wringing Christians! We must pray strongly and confidently! We are not just left here alone, to muddle through the best we can. God is alive and able to do mighty deeds for those who love and obey Him! Let's raise our prayers over our heads and press them deep into the holy ground that Jesus died to give us!

Prayer of the Day

Dear Heavenly Father,

Thank you for caring and hearing my prayers. Sometimes I have the words to describe what is in my heart and mind, but other times my prayers must sound pitiful. I struggle to find the words, but thank You for just letting me be still under the blanket of Your love and grace. Lord, I will keep praying; I'll keep coming to that holy ground. Help me to accept that I must keep praying even if some of my prayers are not answered in my lifetime.

Give me a greater vision, Lord. Jesus instructed me to pray and I will heed His wise counsel. He knew how integral prayer should be in the lives of all His children. Like the watchful Guide that He is, He knows what I need. How foolish for me to think that I can even face my day without first withdrawing some of the peace and strength Jesus has already deposited for me.

Through prayer I'll learn to rely on You, and through answered prayer I'll begin to understand who I'm becoming in You. I don't fully comprehend how this mystical communication between us works, but I do know it is real and quite miraculous. Amen.

Early Childhood Tip

Try this activity to illustrate to your children how God does answer prayer. You'll be surprised how this simple project will teach your children about God's timing and how creatively God answers our prayers.

Buy an inexpensive notebook with lined paper. With a marker label the front: The _____ Family Prayer Notebook. Open the notebook and position it so the binding is at the top. With a ruler and pen, section your notebook so that there are five columns. Label them:

1. Name of Person
2. Today's Date
3. Prayer
4. How Did God Answer
5. Date of Answered Prayer

When someone in your family, a friend, a neighbor or church member needs prayer, enter it into your family log. For example, you could have an entry like this: In **Column 1)** Uncle Matt. **Column 2)** January 14, 2____. **Column 3)** Uncle Matt needs a new job. He just got laid off. Pray for a new job and patience for Uncle Matt and Aunt Rhonda. (The rest of the entry will stay blank until the prayer is answered.) At that time, continue in **Column 4)** Uncle Matt ran into an old college friend. This friend has offered Uncle Matt a new job. He'll be making more money than at his "old" job and he won't have to work on Sunday evenings anymore, which will allow him to go to evening church services with the family! **Column 5)** February 4, 2____.

Let's look at the wonderful "teachable moments" an entry like this would provide for us. First, it shows your children that not only are you concerned about your little nuclear family, you also have a heart for others—especially when they are going through rough times. Besides praying about Uncle Matt's job situation, you are also praying that he and Aunt Rhonda have patience and trust God through the trial. Point out to your children that Uncle Matt's bad situation actually turned out to be a blessing. Talk about how God arranges situations for us, i.e., Uncle Matt running into an old college friend. Not only will this relative now make more money, he will also be able to attend evening worship with his family. Interesting. Together, praise God for the answered prayer. Children want to help, yet are limited because of their age, size and resources. Prayer, however, is something they can do for anyone! This will boost their self-esteem. They will be proud to be able to "do something." If they grow up seeing this approach, then later when the storms of life wash over them they'll pray about their problems instead of worrying about them.

When you are setting up your columns be sure to allow lots of room to write down information. Be specific about the prayer request and add as many details as you can, but in a simple, kid-friendly way.

Another example: Let's say your daughter Jenny wants prayer because she's heartsick over her best friend moving away. **Column 1)** Jenny. **Column 2)** March 22, 2----. **Column 3)** Jenny's best friend, Amy, is moving to another part of the country. Pray that Jenny and Amy will be able to stay close through letters and phone calls. Pray that God will comfort them through the difficult separation, and perhaps enable them to see each other sometime in the future. **Column 4)** Amy called today! Her family is coming back to our hometown for a family reunion. She can stay at our house for three whole days! **Column 5)** August 5, 2----.

Notice that there will be times, as in this entry, when there will be substantial time between the prayer date and the answered prayer. Children will see that God doesn't forget them. He loves them and cares about the things going on in their lives. God is working behind the scenes on our behalf.

However, there will be sections left blank in your family prayer log. Talk about how certain prayers may not be answered for many, many years, and that this can be frustrating to us.

Keep your prayer journals. As your children grow and mature in their spiritual journey, they can return to this prayer log and see very practical ways that God answered their prayers!

Chapter 22

The Responsibility of Children

22

A Precious Seedling

WHEN God gives us the awesome blessing of a child, it is like He is giving us a little seedling. He doesn't give us an adult tree, He gives us a small, frail seedling. We must make many decisions in order to care for this little sapling. This blessing is both a privilege and a responsibility.

We could just plant the seedling anywhere—after all, it would still grow. It would be okay. The rain would fall; the sun would shine. The little seedling, with lots of freedom, would grow in the direction of its own choosing. This would produce a very scraggly tree, but hey, it's a tree!

Because no "real" thought was given to its direction, it would probably do some early forking. Its trunk might take on a variety of bends and turns. Its heartwood, the inner core, would show the effects of this indetermination, its quality forever changed. Let's suppose the seedling's caregivers were too busy taking care of their own root systems to worry about the little seedling. Would the seedling grow up straight? Probably not; it would branch out unevenly, due to the divided trunk. But hey, its a tree!

In contrast, if the little seedling were carefully planted in rich soil, close to a constant stream, it would have received daily nourishment. Stable roots would have formed, with strong tendrils carving a path to the life-giving stream. During the early years, someone would likely have cared enough to have provided a prop to hold up the little seedling: perhaps a strong stick would have been placed next to it. The seedling would have been nudged close to the stick and loosely tied to it, so as to not hurt its tender bark—the prop only temporary. A mesh plastic fencing would have been lovingly placed around the base of the young tree so that wild animals might not eat its bark or damage it while in its early years of rapid but vulnerable growth. The seedling's caregivers would have spent a great deal of time tending to the young tree, sometimes removing weeds and briers that would have tried to choke out the little seedling's light.

The tiny shrub may have wanted to break loose at times, the prop and mesh fence chafing it. Yet the young seedling wouldn't have been able to deny the warm sense of safety and security that the supports provided it. Later the prop and fencing would have been unnecessary and would have fallen away. The young tree, now straight and tall, would have developed an inner wood of great value. The taller it grew, the more it would have branched out and expanded to become unique and powerful in the forest canopy. This growing up and branching out would have been easier due to the firm foundation beneath it and the discipline instilled by its attentive caregivers during the seedling years.

Where are we going to plant our kids? I believe God invites us to plant our little seedlings near to Him, the living water. We're encouraged to support them with props—God's values and Word. These are to be administered lovingly, not too tightly. When we reveal Jesus and everything He stands for to our children, it will start to surround them like that mesh fencing. This will help them by fending off the wild animals found in their world—unkind schoolmates, peer pressure, and conformity to a secular world. When armed with the security of God's love and His care, the outside world and its power and draw are diminished greatly.

Right now we hold the seedling in our hands. We have a short window of opportunity. Decisions have to be made. Decisions have to be prayed about. There are no guarantees. We'll likely make plenty of mistakes, but don't you think *we* should do the planting? I'm pretty confident that if we wait too long, or get too busy with our own agenda, the world will be happy to do the planting for us.

Prayer of the Day

Dear Heavenly Father,

I desire to do everything I can for my children. While they are young, I know I have the chance to guide them in Your direction. Help me to show them the relevance of the Bible in our everyday lives as a family. I know, through walking with You, that they won't have true peace and joy in this life without You; but Lord, help me to get that across to them in a gentle, non-judgmental way. Perhaps, if they see that You are *my* constant Guide, they'll want You guiding them in the future. I pray now for my children. I pray that You bless them with wisdom and spiritual maturity beyond their years. Lord, I know You have a plan and a purpose for their lives. I'm not competent for this overwhelming job of parenting these very different kids, but maybe that is exactly where You want me—needy! I must have You, Jesus. I can't do it on my own; I'm not even suppose to try. Amen.

Scripture to meditate on today:

Isaiah 38:19 (TLB)

The living, only the living, can praise you as I do today. One generation makes known your faithfulness to the next.

Psalm 119:49–52 (TLB)

Never forget your promises to me your servant, for they are my only hope. They give me strength in all my troubles; how they refresh and revive me! Proud men hold me in contempt for obedience to God, but I stand unmoved. From my earliest youth I have tried to obey you; your Word has been my comfort.

Isaiah 44:3 (TLB)

For I will give you abundant water for your thirst and for your parched fields. And I will pour out my Spirit and my blessings on your children.

Psalm 96:12–13 (TLB)

Praise him for the growing fields, for they display his greatness. Let the trees of the forest rustle with praise.

Early Childhood Tip

• Art Activity •

This is a fun and creative art activity perfect for a crisp autumn day. Pull on your sweaters and take along your camera and a paper bag for each child. If you don't have trees in your yard or neighborhood, I suggest driving to a nearby park so you can collect a variety of tree leaves for this activity. Invite your children to gather a variety of colors, types and sizes, and place them in their leaf bag. Put your children's names on the outside of the bags with a large black magic marker. Take any opportunity you can to expose them to their name in written form. Name recognition will be one of the first things your child's preschool teacher will work on. If you start working on it now, they'll be able to recognize their name on their cubby, their crayon box, etc.

As they begin to get into this leaf collecting, snap a few unposed photos. Some of my best photos of my children are those taken while they were playing in a pile of leaves. Relax and enjoy the day.

Talk about the changing seasons with your children. Point out that the leaves from different trees do not look the same. Ask them the colors of the leaves. Crunch some leaves in your hands, close to their ear, and talk about our sense of hearing. Compare a dry leaf and a moist leaf. Touch the bark of the trees. Show them how the old trees are fat and wide. Try to get your arms around them. Compare the young and old trees. "Can we gently shake a young tree? What about an old one?" Try it. Point out that some trees have needles and some bear nuts. Some are special because they have a bird or squirrel nest resting in their branches.

Before you go inside, sit down with your children under a tree. Put one of them in your lap and pray out loud. It is right for them to hear you worshiping and talking to the Lord. Thank Him for the beauty of the earth and the trees. You are a model: Model genuine prayer. Model genuine thankfulness.

Later, when inside, cover the kitchen table with newspaper or use your "art activity/trashable" tablecloth. Give your children each a piece of large white paper. On each paper write the child's name, saying each letter out loud as you write it. Spread the leaves out onto a tray. Ask your children to match the leaves by putting them in groups—all the oak leaves in one pile, for example. Matching is an essential reading-readiness activity. Put some glue onto a plate and provide a wet paper towel for each child.

Flip the papers over to the front and invite each child to make a leaf picture. Tell them they can make a design or even a leaf person, a leaf house, a leaf robot, a leaf car, etc. They'll come up with all sorts of great ideas. They can tear the leaf if they need smaller pieces. Instruct them to make their design first, placing the leaves on the white paper and moving them around to achieve the desired arrangement. When they are happy with their design, start the gluing process by putting glue onto the back of each leaf. The wet paper towel is for the sticky fingers.

To give their pictures a "finished look" give the children a rubber stamp depicting a leaf, and a copper or gold stamp pad so each one can stamp a border around the edge of his paper.

After your photos from your leaf walk are developed, staple a cute picture onto the corner of each masterpiece and display their artwork. Because the leaves will dry out and crack, this particular artwork will probably have a short "showing" at the refrigerator gallery. However, you'll have the photos to document your fall day together.

Chapter 23

Marriage

23

Going to the Chapel

*Marriage is an adventure in cooperation.
The more we share the richer we will be;
the less we share the poorer we will be.*
—Harold B. Walker

WHEN I finish a chapter for this book, I place it on Rob's (my husband's) desk and he goes over it with his nasty red pen and checks my grammar and sentence structure. I guess he is my pre-editor, and to tell you the truth, I think he likes his red pen a little too much. Now as I get ready to write this chapter, I realize that since this chapter is going to be about Rob and our marriage, things may get a little innnnnnnnterestinnnng! I have visions of my pre-editor using this chapter along with the kindling for our next fire. Would he? I can also see him giving it back to me with red marks on every sentence to match his angry red face! Still, I will be brave and bold, and try to get this chapter to you, friend.

Do you ever wonder what God was thinking when He put you and your husband together? I sure have. Rob and I are opposites, but I think most marriages are that way. I'm a morning person, Rob is a night owl. I'm organized and a planner, Rob is the "absent-minded professor" and laid back. I'm fast, he's slow. The list goes on and on. If you read books and magazine articles about marriage they will support the idea that the fact that your spouse is so different from you is the thing that *attracted* you to him in the first place. It's only after time, and the stress of everyday living, that those very same things that we once loved begin to drive us nuts!

Well, I guess the Lord knew Rob would start driving me nuts, because God planned something in my life to remind me (visually) that I made a commitment to this wonderful and exasperating man. We live on the beautiful campus of a private school outside Baltimore. My husband is a teacher in the Upper School and I once taught in the Lower School. The school provides reasonable on-campus housing for anyone on the staff. My husband has lived on the campus his entire life. (Both of his parents taught at the school.) I call him "John Boy" because I joined him here on "Walton's Mountain" when we married 16 years ago.

Anyway, the jewel of the campus is the lovely stone chapel that sits on a hill. You can't take your eyes off it as you drive up the tree-lined main drive. Well, I guess that was God's point—because for the last 16 years I have lived in a variety of apartments and homes on the campus. And they all had one thing in common: from a window of every single home that we've occupied you can see that lovely chapel. Rob and I were married in that chapel many years ago. Now if YOU would return to the place where YOU married YOUR husband, wouldn't YOUR heart melt a little? Just looking at the place would flood your mind and heart with precious memories of that "special" day, and how perfect he was, right? Well, I hate that!! Every time I'm mad at him, I don't get to storm around the house thinking awful thoughts about him for very long before I glance out of the window and see the chapel! Does God have my number or what?! He knew I would be so pitiful at this marriage thing and need so much direction on how to *appreciate* my marriage that He placed me right next door to the chapel for the last six of those 16 years! Right next door!!

Like every marriage, ours has had its share of ups, downs, and stages—each stage different and challenging. Every marriage is a *blend*. He brings stuff from his personality, family and past, and I bring stuff from mine. I wanted our blend to be like Chex mix—you know, different but all the flavors blending well. I had great expectations. Didn't you? I didn't realize how hard and how much work this marriage thing would be. Not a clue.

The courtship, engagement, and first years of marriage are relatively easy and carefree. Add a few pregnancies, kids, bills, a house to run, etc., and you then enter the stage where you and your husband feel more like "roommates" than lovers. How did it get so hard? The only time you talk to each other is to discuss who paid what bill and who is picking up which kid from the birthday party. So even though Rob and I had a good marriage, it was suffering from neglect and we had reached a dark stage. I felt neglected and underappreciated. Rob felt overwhelmed and thought I was trying to boss him around too much. If you are at this "place" right now, hold on.

I realized I was not enjoying the journey. I was just trying to endure every day. One morning I asked myself, "When am I planning on enjoying my marriage and my life? When we have more spare time?" (That will never happen.) "When the kids are older?" (Each age has its own demands.) "When we have more money?" (I should not hold my breath on that one! The stock market could crash.) "When? When? When?" The Holy Spirit convicted me that I needed to enjoy my marriage and my life *right now*.

First, I needed to let my husband know how I was feeling. I did. Then I stopped trying to change him and I worked on changing myself and my attitudes. I also made a decision to start appreciating our differences. (God is even showing me how to be *thankful* for them.) I realized our home life is a lot more fun because of our differences. We both were guilty of taking each other for granted. I also realized that I was angry at Rob but not praying for him. Changing Rob's heart and attitudes is God's job, not mine. I prayed that he would begin to appreciate our marriage again. (Oh no, I feel a red-pen edit coming on that one. You'll probably never read that sentence. Darn!)

I found the appropriate scripture in Ecclesiastes 4:12: "Though one may be overpowered, two can defend themselves. A cord of three strands is not quickly broken." This verse reminds us that marriage is about companionship. I married Rob because I wanted to share my life with him. The important third strand here is *God*. God must be in our marriages, actively, if they are going to stand against all the things that could easily break them up. If we let Him, God will help us to find patience with one another. He'll enable us to see the selfishness in our own lives and help us put our spouse first.

God will give us wisdom when our marriage goes through those long periods of imbalance. Like when we're nursing our babies and don't want to be touched—that is a period of imbalance, but it won't last. Wait! Or times when your husband is going through a particularly difficult season at work and is ignoring you—that is a period of imbalance, but it won't last. Wait! Your stressful times will be different than mine, but we all have them. Remember, stressful times will not last forever! We can't control them, but we can control our reaction to them.

It's during these stressful times that Satan attacks us. Believe me, I know. He'll try to convince us that our spouse doesn't care anymore, or try to make us feel sorry for ourselves or mad that we're stuck in this situation. We may even daydream about being with others, or envy those who are single and carefree. When those thoughts come we should quickly seize them and get rid of them, before they take a strong hold on our minds, which is precisely Satan's desire. When my babies would get their hands near the wires during their crawling days, I would quickly smack their hands away. I didn't want them to get hurt. They were in dangerous territory. *Protect your mind.* I know this might sound funny, but smack away those thoughts when they pop into your head. Get out of dangerous territory. Thoughts can be very powerful and play with your emotions. Don't ignore the Holy Spirit's "check" on your life. The Holy Spirit was placed inside you to lead you to understanding and the truth! Capture the good, positive thoughts.

My favorite store at the mall is the candle shop. Anyone who knows me well knows that I love candles. I have them all over my house. I love the warmth and delicate scent that they add to our home. My marriage is a lot like the scented candles I enjoy. My husband is the strong glass jar. He is dependable and sturdy as he holds me, yet soot from the smoke darkens the jar at the top sometimes, preventing me from seeing the inside clearly. He hides his emotions from me. I desperately want to see into his heart. Men! I'm the wife. I'm the wax in the jar—giving of herself, colorful, malleable; sometimes soft as liquid and at other times hard and unbending; illuminating and scented. Women! God . . . God is the wick. If He is not in the center of this, the light will not shine, the fragrance will not escape, and the warmth will not be known and shared.

I want to encourage you to fight for your marriage. It is an unfinished project. How you finish it will be up to you. I have many unfinished projects at my house; I'm sure you have a few also. Regret washes over me when I am reminded of them. There is a large blank canvas sitting in the garage—I was going to paint a picture for our home. *Unfinished.* I planned on making cute Easter sweatshirts with fabric paint for the girls one spring. The sweatshirts are sizes 2 and 4: my girls are currently wearing sizes 10 and 12. *Unfinished.* I have, however, a few finished projects. With the help of a dear friend, I knitted an Icelandic sweater for my husband. I'm so proud of it! I love to see him wearing it. A few years ago, after our third child was born, I trained and ran in a ten-mile race. That was difficult and took a lot of training time. I urge you, look around—look at the projects in your life: some are unfinished and make you sad, and others are finished and make you proud. Your marriage is important. Which category will your marriage fall under? Fight to make it to the *finish line.* You might trip, but get back up and try again. Realizing that you both need God is a sign of strength, not weakness. Let Him and His work be your therapy and counsel. You and your husband don't need to become more religious or join the perfect church. Just put your relationship with *Christ* first. Don't give up on this project— your marriage.

1 John 2:16–17
> *For everything in the world—the cravings of sinful man, the lust of his eyes and the boasting of what he has and does—comes not from the Father but from the world. The world and its desires pass away, but the man who does the will of God lives forever.*

When we as a couple are "in the world" the three strands of the marriage cord become frayed and fragile. "The cravings of sinful man" really means anything that the flesh lusts after. Wives sometimes become out of balance with eating and shopping. Men become out of balance with sports and drinking. We sometimes use drugs and porn to escape. We become lazy with our comfortable lives. These things feel good to our flesh; they can also destroy marriages. "The lust of his eyes" could be described in one 30-second commercial: we lust after new clothes, fast cars, decorated homes and shiny boats. Things become too important. "The boasting of what he has and does" erodes our once-pristine marriages by causing us to become workaholics and ignore our spouse. The status and power of our careers become addictive to us.

It breaks my heart to see the contrast of a new marriage and one broken by divorce. When the gold bands were slipped on young, slim fingers, the couple's hearts were addicted to each other. They were happy with a bare apartment and a bed. They were driven not by power or money, but to finding new ways to enjoy each other. All of that has been replaced by things of the world! They gave up something "real" for other things that will pass away.

Do you remember the words of the Skin Horse to the Velveteen Rabbit?

> "When [someone] loves you for a long, long time—REALLY loves you—then you become Real. . . . Generally, by the time you are Real most of your hair has been loved off, and your eyes drop out and you get loose in the joints and very shabby. But these things don't matter at all, because once you are Real you can't be ugly, except to people who don't understand."*

Prayer of the Day

Dear Father,

Thank You for my marriage. Help me to appreciate it. Remind me, Lord, of all the wonderful qualities my husband possesses. I lift up the mothers who are reading this book. I pray that every mom will pause and look, really look, at her wedding band today. Father, she'll see that it has lost some of its shine and it may have a few dents and scratches too. Her marriage has survived some scratches and scrapes over the

---

* Margery Williams, *The Velveteen Rabbit: Or, How Toys Become Real* (New York: Henry Holt, 1999), pp. 4–5.

years and at times the sparkle seems to have dimmed, but, oh, I pray that she will see that her wedding band is still a perfect circle. It is not broken. It is still strong. It was placed there by the man who stole her heart. And the ring was blessed by a God who loves her beyond compare. The marriage is yet unfinished, and she has a God who desires to help her finish things in an excellent way if she'll only trust and let Him be involved. I pray that she'll remember that You are a God of second, third, . . . unending chances, and that each day is a new start.

Early Childhood Tips

Kissing, Praying, and Parables

Tip 1. Kiss and hug your spouse in front of your children. I remember how I loved to see my folks hug or kiss in front of me. It made me feel secure. Many of your children's classmates are from broken homes and are dealing with the fallout of a divorce. Our little ones must sometimes wonder if it'll happen to their own family. Our words can assure them, but why not let our actions seal it with a kiss.

Tip 2. Sometimes you can't help it, you just get ahead of yourself and worry about your child's future. This happens to me when I'm tucking my children into their beds. They smell so sweet. The gentle soapy smell from their bath is still clinging to their skin and fine hair. You place a kiss on their forehead, and you wish the kiss could be a complete stamp of protection against all the horrible things out there in the world that will come against them someday. Your heart just aches for them to be able to find happiness.

I want them to meet and marry the man or woman that God has chosen for them. My children are young, but I am already praying for them and their future marriages. I'm praying that my children will have wisdom in choosing the right person and bypassing all the wrong people that they will meet. I'm praying now that they will grow in discernment so that by the time they are in their late teenage years, they will be able to recognize the qualities important in a lifetime partner. I believe that God has a partner already picked out for them. I choose to not worry about these things, but instead to pray about them. I can tell my kids my opinions and encourage them to take seriously the task of selecting a husband or wife, but will they really listen to me? Only God can work in their hearts and minds.

We as parents can and should pray over these issues. I believe God will honor our prayers. We worry about preparing them for the SATs and getting them into a good college. We worry about their future job security. But college goes by quickly, a job is a job—but their marriage will hopefully last their entire life. Begin tonight to pray for those future marriages.

Tip 3. (ages 8 and up)

How will our children understand the parables of the New Testament? We learn best if we have experience, don't we? Jesus loved to tell stories. He used everyday language to teach higher ways and to enable people to see themselves in situations. By telling our children stories with deeper meanings we will help prepare their little minds to understand the more complex stories (parables) of the Bible.

I tell my children that God has a husband or wife already chosen for them. I made up this short story to illustrate my point. Don't wait until your children are teenagers to start talking to them about dating and marriage. Plant the seeds early. They may not understand all of it right now, but they will see that God is in control and has a plan for their life. They will have hope for their future. And they will understand that you are available to help them cross into adulthood. (If you are telling this story to your son, then obviously change the gender and change the dress in the story to a "hot car" and adjust the story accordingly.)

There once was a young girl at the entrance to a large department store. A kind clerk met her just before she entered and pulled her aside. The clerk opened a book, studied it, closed it, and encouraged the girl to walk to the back of the store. The clerk assured the girl that there was a beautiful dress waiting for her in the back of the store. You could tell by the gleam in the clerk's eyes that she had seen the dress; and by the way she enthusiastically described the handmade, fit-to-perfection garment. The girl could also tell that the clerk had gone through the store herself and had some experience. The girl seemed excited, yet surprised, for she did not remember having any fittings (measurements) taken for the preparation of such a fine dress.

Anxious to get her foot in the store, the young girl took a step forward. The clerk stepped in front of her and warned her, "Look at the other dresses in the store, but don't try them on and don't take too long getting to the back of the store." The girl assured her that she would wait for the dress in the back of the store. The clerk squeezed her hand, then disappeared, and the girl was left alone. She began her journey. She passed many fine-looking dresses. Some were displayed so nicely. But when she took a closer look at some of them she realized they were not as nice as she first thought they were. Some of the dresses had holes in them and were falling apart. Then she came to some sections of the store that were empty, so she walked through them. It took some time, but she finally made it to the back of the store. Her eyes could not *believe* the beautiful dress that was waiting for her! Tears ran down her cheeks as she tried on the dress. It fit her perfectly. She was so glad that she had waited and not tried on the other dresses, for they could not come close to the one designed especially for her.

Encourage a discussion about the story above. Tell your children that this story is really about dating and marriage. They may look confused at first, but lead them into understanding by saying, "This story may appear to be about a dress, but it is really about waiting for the right husband, not the right dress. Someday you'll start dating boys, and there will be many to choose from. The girl in the story was told to look at all the other dresses but to wait for the special dress in the back. God desires for you to marry the man He has planned for you, but He will not force you to wait for that one. He knows that you may meet other men along the way—just like the girl in the story who saw lots of pretty clothes on the way to the back of the store. Some women decide to live with men to 'try things out.' Some marry the wrong man. They have missed out on God's best for them. They settled for men that weren't fine, even as those dresses in the story weren't fine. In the story, remember, she walked through parts of the store that were empty. There may be a time when you may be alone. But it is better to be alone and waiting than to settle for a man who is not right for you. You'll never really be alone. God will always be with you."

Ask, "Did the girl in the story know when she was standing near the best dress? (Yes, she knew. It fit perfectly.) Do you think God will show you when you have met the man that He has picked out for you? That dress that she found in the back of the store, God made for *her*. He planned it and made it with her in mind. If you trust Him, He will show you and guide you to your heart's desire. God has a partner in mind for you. God knows everything about you and your dreams. Will you trust Him?

"Was the girl in the story excited about entering the store? When you start dating, it will be an exciting time for you, too. Do you think the girl in the story was wise to wait for the best dress? She was also very fortunate to have had that clerk to warn her about what she would see in the store. Don't you think that helped? The clerk kept looking at a book that she had in her hands, didn't she? Well, Daddy and Mommy are like that clerk. We want to be there for you as you start to date. We want to warn you about the "store." We've been through the "store." We went through the dating phase. We want to help and guide you, if you'll let us. And do you know what? The book that Mommy and Daddy look to for help is the Bible. We will study that book and then try to give you good advice, like the clerk in the story. For we love you more than anything and we know that God has a great plan for you!"

Chapter 24

Witnessing

24

The Reason for My Hope

1 Peter 3:14–15: *You are blessed . . . do not be frightened. But in your hearts set apart Christ as Lord. Always be prepared to give an answer to everyone who asks you to give the reason for the hope that you have.*

OVER and over in the Bible we read of the last few years of Jesus' life and how He preached throughout the countryside of Israel. People would flock to hear this "teacher." Many were thirsty for someone to explain the Law to them. But as we flip through the Bible we also read of the times Jesus slipped away from the crowds to be with just a few people, namely his twelve special friends. Jesus shared His life with these disciples. He shared the essence of God. He shared insights, concepts, and promises. Now let's remember, He hand-picked these guys. They were a motley crew. They had many character flaws and problems. If we met them, we would probably say, "Lord, why them? Their lives seem to be a mess." Our Lord is so gifted at making beautiful things out of a mess. Jesus witnessed to many, but His witness to these twelve was truly special.

As a stay-at-home mom, you are stepping out into new territory. Many new mothers feel drawn to Christ. I don't know why, but I can guess. Is it that we now can truly understand sacrificial love? It seems that many mothers experience some sort of rededication to the Lord after giving birth. Could it be that we (as women) are just wired that way? Hmmmm . . . God is so smart.

I *do* know that once you start abiding in the Lord, the natural extension of that is the desire to tell others about Jesus. You can't help it! Witnessing is usually described as the process of proclaiming the Christian faith to non-believers. How does this apply to you and your situation? You are probably planning on staying home and rearing your children until the baby in the family enters school. Many of you will then return to the work force, but some of you will homeschool and may never return to work outside the home. You and God will work out the best plan for your family. I just want to say that I applaud you for choosing to follow your heart. I'm here to encourage you as you swim upstream while everyone else is going downstream. During this period of being a full-time mom, God will place many people in your path. Many of these folks need to hear about the "good news" of Christ. God will provide numerous opportunities for you to witness. Obviously, not everyone you meet or get to know well will be responsive or ready, but don't let that discourage you.

Did you ever hear that "the fruit of a Christian is another Christian"? That is a powerful sentence. Some of you may have a real desire to witness to others, but are unsure about how to take the first step. You are, however, witnessing already! Yes, you are—you are witnessing to your children. Every time you read a Bible story to them, plop in a Christian video or say a prayer, you are witnessing. This is the most important witnessing you will ever, ever do, and most of the chapters in this book are designed to help you specifically with that witnessing relationship. But today I'm talking specifically about witnessing to other people whom God places in your path. It could be your old college friend, a cousin, the new mom in your church play-group, or the guy you always talk to at the dry cleaners.

Does God use you to witness only if you know the entire Bible, walk perfectly in your Christian faith, and always ooze with Christian love? No! No! A thousand times no! I believe that God is looking for people who give Him their lives and their time. The woman who desires to witness understands that she is a sinner and knows that she could not survive one single day without starting and ending the day on her knees. Listen, if we wait until our character is flawless, our flesh not alive and our spirit fully submissive, then we'll never ever witness to anyone! Satan paralyzes many potentially wonderful witnesses for Christ because he lies to them and convinces them that they will look foolish or pushy or stupid. If you truly love God and are a good listener, then you are ready to witness!

First of all, pray and ask the Lord to guide you to people who need to hear about Jesus. Be patient. Build great friendships. Be an excellent listener. People want to talk about their concerns and problems. Win their confidence by listening and caring about what they are going through. Jesus listened and had compassion for His lost sheep (Luke 15). Eventually, God will give you a "window"—a time when you can speak to them about Jesus. I had a close friendship with a man (a high-school buddy) for 18 years before I was able to openly witness to him. We had a solid friendship, but it took time before a "window" opened.

Sometimes, when you try to witness to people, they keep bringing up all their problems (old ones and new ones)! When this happens, write some of them down on a piece of paper and tell your friend that, after you share some good news with him/her, you will return to the paper and pray about all the problems—that, together, the two of you can take the problems to the "problem-solver." This lets your friend know that you legitimize his problems, but you've learned to take them to God. You can, then, move on to talk about God's plan for salvation as a solution to his problems. Stay on track.

Secondly, keep things simple. Do not introduce too much too soon. We can look to Paul as our example. Paul encouraged others in a gentle but persistent manner. He knew he was telling them something powerful and timely. Ask God for wisdom. You will need to try to understand where the friend is in terms of his/her spiritual walk. You have to be prepared to start where that person is. I hope you aren't thinking, "Okay, this is getting too complicated! I'll become tongue-tied. I'll look foolish. I'm going to forget what I wanted to say." Please don't think that. When you step out to tell others about Christ, believe me, Christ will meet you. He will give you the courage. He will give you the words. Trust Him. Let me show you something in the Bible that may inspire you. Acts 4:13 tells us: "When they saw the courage of Peter and John and realized that they were unschooled, ordinary men, they were astonished and they took note that these men had been with Jesus." Your friend will see by the joy on your face and the warmth of your voice that you have been with Jesus also.

Okay, now we have to talk about the "place." The "place"? Yes, the place in the conversation where you bring in spiritual matters. The place where you are going to "do it"—talk about Jesus. The tone of the conversation is going to change. You're going to jump in headfirst, not knowing whether the water will be cold, shallow or rocky. Some people like to begin by sharing their own testimony. You may want to try this approach. Share how your life was before you came to Christ and after you met Him. Share how God has met your needs. Let them in on how God has answered prayer. Tell them the things you still struggle with. Tell them that there are many things that you still don't understand in the Bible, but you keep seeking God's will for your life. Remember, you are not telling them about a formula or a magic cure. You are telling them about a relationship, one that they too can have if only they ask.

A different approach, but one you may find to be more comfortable, would be to ask some deep questions. Here are some examples:

- Do you ever think about spiritual things?
- Has anyone ever taken the time to tell you about Jesus, God's Son?
- If you died tonight, would you go to heaven?
- Did you ever receive Jesus into your heart as your personal Lord and Savior?
- We'll all stand before God one day. If God were to ask you why you should be allowed into heaven, what would you say?
- What hinders you from having a relationship with Christ?

You'll be able to tell right away if their hearts are open to hear about Jesus. Tell them in your own words (with God's help, of course) that God's plan for us is to have peace and life. You might want to say something like this:

"We are all loved by God. But our problem is that we are separated from God because of our sins. God's solution is Jesus. He, the eternal Son, came to earth as a man. Jesus became human like us, but without sin, so we could become like Him and ultimately live in paradise forever. God knew that if He didn't do something—give us a real part of Himself—we would never understand how much

He loved us. Jesus sacrificed His life on the cross to pay the penalty for our sins. He loves you that much! He thinks your life has worth! You can never be good enough to get into heaven. We can never follow all God's laws; we cannot save ourselves. We must accept the free gift of salvation from Jesus. Admit that you are a sinner. Ask Jesus to forgive you and take your life and change you. Yield yourself to God. Decide to not live by your feelings or desires but by the truth of God. Follow Him! Jesus bled on the cross so that we could live with Him in heaven when we die—but that is not *all*. The good news is that He was resurrected to give us peace and victory *now* while we're still here on this crazy earth! His Spirit dwells inside of each saved sinner. He told us He would never leave us, and He hasn't."

You'll be surprised by how many people really want to talk about spiritual things.

Afterwards, go home and read Hebrews 4:12 and pray! Hebrews 4:12: "For the word of God is living and active. Sharper than any double-edged sword, it penetrates even to dividing soul and spirit, joints and marrow; it judges the thoughts and attitudes of the heart." So, even if they look at you with a blank sort of stare, know that later on they will think about what you have said. The word of God is sharp and it goes deep. Lead someone to Jesus. You, of course, won't save them; Christ will do that! You are just an available marker on the road, pointing the way.

Prayer of the Day

My Heavenly Father,

I want to tell others about You. I'm so busy doing my "mommy thing" that sometimes I'm just overwhelmed with all the tasks ahead of me each day. But, Lord, help me to know that those tasks, in themselves, have no eternal value. The time and energy that I put into friends and other people that You have so strategically placed near to me is far more important. How can I keep such wonderful news to myself? Why is it so easy for me to share a yummy recipe, an engaging book, or a fine meal with friends, yet I stay silent about the one thing that has eternal value?

Give me courage. Help me to discern the people that may need to hear about You. Help me to fight past my fear of rejection. Let my life be a witness! Convict me with the knowledge that your Word gives me: that I must witness if I am to call myself Your child. Give me a real heart for people and their problems. Keep me from becoming so involved with my own needs that I don't have grace for others.

There are so many hurting people that need you, Father. Help me to be a faithful servant and to guide them on the path to You. May they see, and may my lips proclaim, that You are all they need. Jesus was crucified, but Jesus is alive, today! Thank You for the privilege of witnessing for You!

Oh, and Jesus, I'm counting on You to continue meeting me at the "place," okay? Amen.

Early Childhood Tip

Let your children know when you have witnessed to someone. When you are having prayers or devotions with your children before bed, explain to them that you would especially like to pray for _____ tonight because you were able to witness to him or her recently. Explain in simple terms what witnessing for Jesus is.

I strongly believe in praying deeply with our children. Soak them with intelligent prayer. Why do we assume they can understand only simple prayers like "Now I lay me down to sleep . . ."? That is crazy! They are much smarter than that. Will they understand everything that you are saying in your prayers? Probably not. But what they will understand is that you are treating prayer as a valuable part of your day. They will see that you have an intimate relationship with God and direct access just by praying. Your children will also understand that you care about the person that you have witnessed to and that now you can "take your hands off" of the situation and lift this person up to God.

Here's another early childhood tip I would like to encourage you to do with your kids. The next time you go over a bridge, whether walking on a woodland trail or crossing over by car, use the bridge as a symbol. Use it as a story starter. You could say something like "This bridge makes me think of Jesus. Do you know why?" then talk about how sinful man is on one side and a holy God is on the other. "We need a bridge don't we? Jesus is the bridge." They'll find this word picture meaningful. Children sometimes grasp spiritual concepts faster than adults! Never underestimate them.

Chapter 25

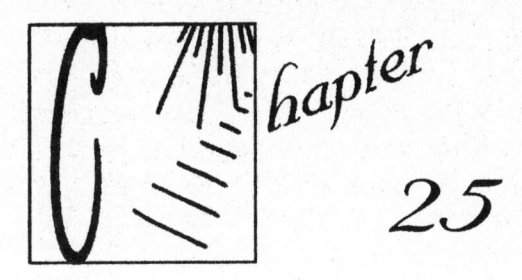

Overcoming and the Names of God

25

You'll Have a New Name

WHEN I married my husband sixteen years ago I was proud to take his name. But I have to admit I was a little attached to my maiden name. My maiden name is Spence. It's a fine English name. I've always thought that it has a nice soft ring to it—unlike my new married name, which was to be Smoot. It rhymes with flute. How such a hard, harsh-sounding name could come from such a pretty place as the Netherlands is beyond me. No one ever mispronounced my maiden name—well, yes once, at my college graduation. But you should hear the interesting pronunciations of my married name: Smooch, Smut and Smooth are a few of my personal favorites. While taking a new name was an adjustment, I knew God had the right idea about this "two-becoming-one thing" and so Smoot it would be. I knew I would get use to it.

Well . . . we had returned from our honeymoon only a few weeks when I made an appointment to see a new doctor for a checkup. I was engrossed in a magazine article when a cheerless nurse walked into the waiting room with a clipboard in hand. She called, "Mrs. Smoot." No response. Again, she tried "Mrs. Smoot," in a louder voice. Finally, I realized that she was calling my new name! I was so embarrassed. I jumped up, threw the magazine aside, and quickly explained that I was unaccustomed to my new married name and flashed my shiny wedding band in front of her as if to prove that I wasn't completely stupid. She rolled her eyes and I thought to myself, Will I ever get used to this new name?

God decided to do some name changing of His own in the Bible. The name change was not made to show a change in marital status but in character status.

In the very first book of the Bible, Genesis, chapter 32, we can read about how Jacob acquired his new name. I don't have any idea what men of that century took for an upset stomach or a panic attack, but whatever it was, I'm sure Jacob was searching the four corners of his tent to find some. Imagine that you are just about to see your brother, Esau, for the first time in many years. The last time you saw him he wanted to kill you because you had deceived him and stolen your father Isaac's patriarchal blessing!

The name Jacob means "he grabs the heel" or "he deceives," and Jacob was living up to that name rather nicely. Power and money belonged to Jacob, but something eluded him that all of his wealth could not buy—reconciliation with his brother.

Just as God allows intense sandstorms in the hot desert to carve new dunes and erase once-traveled roads, God was allowing storms into Jacob's life to cut new paths and eliminate old patterns. The "deceiver" was now wrestling with God. This wrestling match was a turning point for Jacob, but, like in most things, it was probably a culmination of many little spiritual journeys. Each journey provided Jacob with a piece of the puzzle. This stirring wrestling with God was perhaps the time when the pieces started to fall into place. Jacob was beginning to let God rule over all of his decisions—all of his life. How blessed we are to have a God who cares enough about us individually to wrestle with us about ourselves and our character!

Genesis 32:28: "Then the man [God appearing as an angel] said, 'Your name will no longer be Jacob, but Israel, because you have struggled with God and with men and have overcome.'" God saw a change in Jacob's character and presented him with a new name. I love the way God honored Jacob's brokenness and humility by softening Esau's heart and allowing the brothers to reconcile soon afterward.

It's almost as if Jacob knew the names of God but, until this pivotal point, hadn't bothered to delve deeper (on a personal level) to understand the awesome meaning of those names. Jacob knew that God had called himself, "The God of your fathers Abraham and Isaac." Didn't Jacob, Abraham's very own grandson, see the pattern of sovereignty in that name? He was also aware of God's other name,

"Yahweh—the Mighty I Am." Couldn't Jacob feel the omnipresent power in the syllables of that name? Jacob, the parent of eleven sons (at that time) and one daughter, knew how to be a father. God had to teach him how to be a son of the *heavenly* Father. Is God trying to teach us as well, to behold the power and promise that we have in His Name?

This name-change story took place in the first book of the Bible, Genesis. But there are some relevant connections with the very last book of the Bible, which is Revelation. Again we hear about overcoming.

This verse describes things to come. Revelation 2:17: "To him who overcomes [i.e., believers in Christ], I [God] will give some of the hidden manna. I will also give him a white stone with a new name written on it, known only to him who receives it." I think we should find great hope in both Jacob's Genesis verse and this Revelation verse. The Christian life is not going to be an easy one. Being a strong Christian mother is not going to be easy in the world we live in today. We are told from the beginning of the Bible that we will have to overcome, but are encouraged that there will be a reward at the end. The help we need for the "unwelcome, overcoming part" is found sandwiched in between Genesis and Revelation. All those books filled with stories of imperfect people, psalms of hope and warnings of pitfalls, are there to help and to encourage us along the way.

There is one more name that we must take a look at. It's found in the opening chapter of Revelation, where we hear Jesus called "The Faithful Witness" (Rev. 1:5). This is the only time in the Bible that He is called by that name. When I think of a witness I immediately think of a trial. We don't know the full meaning behind the white stones with our new names on them, but white stones were once used in ancient courts. Do you know what they were used for? They declared an *acquittal* verdict.

Acquittal means the freeing of a person from an accusation of wrongdoing. Could that be why we'll be given a white stone? Does it represent our own acquittals? Jesus took our sentences. He was our witness and declared our innocence with His blood. He paid the price for all of our wrongdoings—past, present and future—when He died on the cross.

In our heavenly home, we'll finally have the character we've always wanted but couldn't attain in our earthly bodies. It'll be our turn for a new name! The overcoming and the wrestling will be over!

Our new names will be written on pure white stones. And this time, I'll have an eternity to get used to the new name!

Other Scripture to meditate on today:

Revelation 3:5
He who overcomes will, like them, be dressed in white. I will never blot out his name from the book of life, but will acknowledge his name before my Father and his angels.

Psalm 99:3
Let them praise your great and awesome name—he is holy.

Matthew 6:9
Our Father in heaven, hallowed be your name, your kingdom come, your will be done on earth as it is in in heaven.

Prayer of the Day

Dear Father,

Sometimes I forget that great men of faith are not born as such. Jacob, who was born into the "religious First Family," still had to grow into his faith, as all followers must. As I meditate on all of Your names, it just reminds me of how wise and loving You are to Your children. You are Creator, Provider, Helper, Presence, Breath, the Vine, the Light, the Way, the Truth, and the Life. You left nothing out. No father loved his children more than You do. Thank You for sending Jesus so that we may experience the reality of Your character. Help us to overcome. There has never been a sweeter NAME than the name Jesus. Amen.

Early Childhood Tip

• Stone Art •

You'll need:
- a variety of stone/rock sizes*
- paint
- brushes
- smocks or old clothes
- glue

Make a stone family that looks like your family. You can do this yourself and surprise everyone, or else you can have everyone in the family make their own. Paint a face on a round flat-looking stone. Next, paint a larger stone to look like an outfit: shirt and shorts for a boy stone-person, a dress or skirt and top for a girl stone-person. Choose four long, flat stones for the arms and legs. Don't forget to paint on shoes and socks. The rocks that are depicting the arms could be holding something like flowers, a ball or a briefcase. Be creative. Try to make your stone-person show the personality of the family member it's depicting.

Glue your stone-person together and cover with a coat of shellac. Place it somewhere outside, where it'll be enjoyed and appreciated by your family and visitors. You might want to place it flat on the ground near a large planter filled with flowers that you have sitting beside the front door.

When I did this with my family, we put each family member's name on another rock alongside their stone-person.

---

* If you can't find flat rocks or pebbles near your home, try a gardening/craft store.

Chapter 26

Strangers

26

The Filing Cabinet

I NEVER planned on writing this chapter. But I realize now that I must include it and that it may be the most important chapter in the entire book.

A parent's worst nightmare is the thought of his/her child being abducted and hurt by a stranger. According to the website www.safewithin.com, there are more than 100,000 attempted abductions reported each year! Most parents tell their children to be wary of strangers. They spend a little time warning their kids about the potential danger, but they usually feel it's information that they'll probably never have to put into use. I hope after reading this chapter you'll be inspired to do everything in your power to educate your little ones about malicious strangers. I know you think it'll never happen to you—not in your neighborhood. I thought that, too. But it almost happened to my children, right in front of my home. And it could happen to your children.

Sickened by newspaper articles describing how young children were being lured and then molested by adults, I decided as a classroom teacher many years ago to include a unit of study about "strangers." During our classroom discussions, I gave the children in my class some hypothetical situations with strangers. My plan was to create a little filing cabinet inside each child's brain. My prayer was that it would never have to be opened and that they would never have to use any of the information I was filing away. Regardless, folders of *awareness*, not fear, were filed in their little filing cabinets as we discussed places to avoid, appropriate words to say to strangers, and how to react keenly to situations.

Of course, when I traded chalk dust for baby-powder dust, I did my own little unit on "strangers" with my three children. I was looking forward to adding Christian elements into the conversation that I couldn't use in the classroom setting. I hope you are seeing a common thread throughout this book. Everything we teach our children can be an opportunity to incorporate Jesus and our faith. It is my hope that we never compartmentalize Jesus and talk of Him only on Sundays or only at church. Children who have a mother who brings Jesus into their everyday experience will naturally come to see God as involved, trustworthy, and real! Our children will never embrace our values and faith because we force them to or stick it down their throats every Sunday, but when they see that following Christ helps us to make sense of this crazy world, our faith will pass down to them.

I started out by telling my children that most people (almost all adults) love children. I assured them that most adults do everything they can to care for and help little children. But we must warn our children that there are some people who don't have Jesus in their heart. Because of that, some of them are unkind and they sometimes take and hurt children. I know this sounds harsh. But we need to warn them about the real world. I hate to hasten their knowledge of the ugly side of life—it comes soon enough. But we have to remember that "sick people" who abduct children are counting on us to not warn our children, making it easier for them to be lured away. I'm grateful that I did not candycoat this for my three children; it may have saved their lives.

For Christian moms, this provides us a perfect opportunity to give our children a glimpse of heaven. Why shouldn't we continually compare this place (our temporary home) to our real home (heaven)? I always tell my kids that heaven is their "real home" and that we're just passing through. Tell them that in heaven there won't be unkind and cruel strangers who hurt children, but that they do exist in *this* world. By explaining to your children that God is allowing humans to choose goodness or darkness, you are pouring a foundation for deeper spiritual understanding later about free will. So, encourage your children to be "homesick" for heaven. Give them hope! Let them know this isn't all there is! Do you realize how influential we can be as moms? We need to plant the seeds of hope!

Talk about what your children should do and say if they are approached by a stranger at the playground, the store, or at a sporting event (common hangouts for child abductors). Relate that sometimes it is okay to say "No!" to an adult and to run away. In some cases it is not disrespectful. Following orders from strangers is something they do *not* have to do! Instruct your children to yell if someone grabs them. In that case, it is appropriate to scream, *"This is not my Daddy (or Mommy)! Help!"* Spend time explaining that bad strangers can look nice and dress well. They are not always messy and ugly like on television or videos. Stress that a bad person may not always be a man. Sometimes women accost children, or work together with men. The more your kids know, the more confident they'll be in a variety of situations. Make files for their filing cabinet! Add files! Knowledge and preparation empowers us at any age.

Next, get specific. The lies that sick and abusive adults use to lure children away are clever and take advantage of a child's natural sense of helpfulness and compassion. Strangers may lie and say . . .

"I'm lost; can you get in the car and give me a few directions while I write them down?"

"I have a cane (or wheelchair) because my leg is hurt. Could you just open my car door for me?"

"I have some new bikes in my garage that I don't need anymore. Would you like to pick out one to keep?"

"Your parents called me. They were in a car accident and are waiting for you at the hospital. Get in and I'll be glad to take you to them."

"I'm making a movie and we need some children for one of the scenes. You are so pretty. Would you like to be in a show?"

"I've lost my new puppy (or kitty). Could you please help me look for it? I'm sure it is scared and hungry."

It's shocking to me that what were meant to be brilliant and creative adult minds—that could have been used mightily for the Lord—could turn away from the light of God. Instead, through rebellion and Satan's influence, these minds are used for such evil against precious little children.

It is much too vague to say, "Don't talk to strangers." These men and women are often professionals and are extremely cunning. But kids can be prepared for the tricks and emotion-packed lies of the stranger.

Little did I know that one spring Saturday afternoon my children would be confronted by one of the very lies that I had warned them about. The filing cabinet was yanked wide open.

It is now necessary to backtrack a few weeks. That would be to the day when my 12-year-old, the one who is antsy to start her own babysitting empire, was making me feel guilty about being the only mom in the neighborhood who accompanies her children EVERYWHERE! So after a refresher course on "strangers," I cut the apron strings a little and allowed Brielle to take her sister, 10, and brother, 7, on short jaunts to the playground, which is three houses away from our home. After all, our neighborhood is on the campus of a private school. Everyone knows everyone.

It was Brielle, Brandy and Hunter's third solo trip to the playground. I was at home working on this book. Spring had definitely sprung in Baltimore and it was one of those perfect spring days. Mowers were humming. Bright yellow daffodils dotted the yard; they were waving in the breeze as if to brag about being first. We all seemed to be suffering from severe cases of "spring fever." I was glad the children could finally get outside in the fresh air.

It was 2:00 on a Saturday afternoon. They were at the playground for an hour. Then I heard the front door slam, and the "Moooooom!" that you don't want to hear rang in my ears. It had a tinge of fear and hurt trailing behind it.

Brielle's face was flushed, and she paced as she tried to tell me what had just happened. An older man in a pickup truck had pulled up beside the children as they were walking the short distance home from the playground. Brielle noticed that this man had a wheelchair folded up and lying in the bed of his truck. He asked them if they had seen a kitten and went on to explain that he had lost his.

"Mom, I remembered what you told us about strangers lying about needing help to find their lost cat or dog!" she exclaimed as she looked at me with disbelief. "He looked at us in a weird way, too!" she continued. After the stranger asked Brielle about the kitten, she said "No!" and, quickly grabbing her brother and sister, moved far away from the truck, ran towards our front door, and hurried inside and locked the door. The stranger was brazen enough to follow the children down the road and turn around in our driveway before leaving!

I couldn't believe it! My husband arrived home minutes later. In fact, now I'm pretty sure that Rob must have actually passed the stranger in the pickup truck as he was leaving the street and neighborhood. Our street is a dead end. I grabbed a pen and a piece of paper and jumped in the car with Brielle, leaving the other children at home with my husband. We drove all over the area. I hoped to spot the truck and perhaps write down its license plate. Unfortunately, the truck and the stranger were gone.

That Sunday, instead of reading the church bulletin and looking at the pastor, I was reading a police report and looking at mug shots! I hated the fact that my children had to go through such a frightening ordeal, but I was extremely proud of the way that they had handled the situation.

I felt so violated. I hated the fact that this wacko knew where my children lived and that he knew their beautiful faces. I felt so many emotions. I felt fearful, angry, and very vulnerable. I wanted to move. I couldn't walk through the house without looking out of the windows towards the driveway for a pickup truck. "What if he comes back?" I wondered. I just couldn't believe how close my children had come to being taken from me. If they had helped him, perhaps he would have grabbed them and well . . . the "what ifs" were driving me crazy.

So here I was in the middle of writing a Christian devotional and finding myself paralyzed with fear. I decided I needed to read my own book—to read the advice I've been giving you and run to the shelter of God.

I spent a wonderful time in prayer with God. I praised Him over and over for protecting my children. I chastised myself for all the "what ifs" coming from my mouth. I prayed that God would help me to trust in His care over my children. I also started praying for the man—the stranger.

I prayed for my enemy. Oh, I've read about loving my enemies. I've taught a youth group lesson on loving your enemies. My Sunday school classes heard me talk about it. As a Billy Graham counselor I've counseled many people about it, but God was touching my heart to make me actually do it! I knew that this man must have had some problems in his life that kept him from having appropriate loving relationships. I prayed for him. I prayed that the memory of this day and my children's beautiful faces would be totally erased from his mind. Some people will read this and say, "Elizabeth, that would take a miracle." I know that. But I serve a God who performs miracles every day. As soon as I started praying for the man, I began to have peace. I didn't have the urge to check the doors and windows three times a day or sleep on the floor of my children's room at night. I could walk by the windows and not look for a pickup truck. Besides praying myself, I also called my Christian friends and my pastor, and asked them to be covering my children and home in prayer.

I searched my Bible for scriptures on fear and was led to some that described my feelings so perfectly. It really is the best self-help book.

2 Timothy 1:7 (NKJV)
For God has not given us the spirit of fear, but of power and of love and of a sound mind.

Psalm 56:4
In God, whose word I praise, in God I trust; I will not be afraid. What can mortal man do to me?

Psalm 31:20–21 (TLB)
Hide your loved ones in the shelter of your presence, safe beneath your hand, safe from all conspiring men. Blessed is the Lord, for he has shown me that his never-failing love protects me like the walls of a fort!

Psalm 31:1–2,4 (TLB)
Lord, I trust in you alone. Don't let my enemies defeat me. Rescue me. . . . Answer quickly when I cry to you; bend low and hear my whispered plea. Be for me a great Rock of safety from my foes. Pull me from the trap my enemies have set for me. For you alone are strong enough.

This "stranger" incident was in some ways an end to my children's innocence. I had talked and warned them about something that we all thought would never happen. Yet it became very real, with real police interviews, etc. Now my kids know firsthand that bad people are out there; but they showed me by their calmness during and after the event that they have a strong confidence in God's love and care for them.

Brandy, my ten-year-old, hugged me and said, "Oh Mommy, it's going to be okay. God had lots of angels watching over us." I think I understand why the Bible tells us to have childlike faith.

One night, shortly after the incident, I was curled up on the bed with all three of them. We prayed together. We thanked God for Brielle's clear head. We prayed for the stranger. We prayed that he would not try to take any other children. We prayed that he would come to know the Lord and change his life. I can't tell you how this helped us. We just gave it all to the Lord—our fears, our praise, our hopes. God honored us with a sense of peace and calmness immediately. It was the best prayer time I've ever had with my children. What Satan means for our harm, God will turn it into something good.

Please talk to your children about strangers. Don't wait. Do it today. It may be one of the most important conversations that you'll ever have with them. Moms, do some filing; but hope and pray that they never have to open the filing cabinet drawer. Yet if they do, it'll be there—stocked with lots of good information and completely stuffed with God's love and protection.

Prayer of the Day

Dear Heavenly Father,

Thank You for the protection that You daily lavish on my family. It's a constant care that I never want to take for granted. Give me, as a mother, the peace of knowing that when my eyes are off my children, Yours are still there. Thank You for replacing my fear with trust through prayer and Your calming Word. You are showing me, through this situation, my utter dependence on You. That doesn't make me weaker, only stronger.

Why was I looking out into the driveway the first 24 hours in fear? Why wasn't I looking inward, to the Holy Spirit, to find You?

Right after the children told me what had happened, I hugged them tighter than I've ever hugged them. I didn't want to ever release them. The thought of losing them was just too painful to bear. In that moment, Lord, You put everything in my life into perspective. My most precious things were in my arms. I finally understand the love it took for You to release Your child, Jesus. Thank You. Amen.

Early Childhood Tip

I don't know about you, but my purse seems to stay organized for only about two days, tops. As hard as I try, I can't seem to eliminate items from the collection. My mother always teases me that it feels more like a suitcase than a purse, and she's right; but you never know when you'll need that shiny matchbox car or the tin of mints. Moms just have a lot of stuff that they need to *survive*!

That is why you'll probably cringe when I suggest that you add some more things to the abyss made of leather that you hang on your shoulder. Your husband needs to carry this in his wallet at all times too. What I'm proposing is that all parents carry an envelope that you will hopefully never need—but it could save the lives of your children.

The envelope should contain two photos of your child: A close-up front view and a close-up profile (side-view). If you are lucky enough to have a scanner, scan the pictures and include these in the envelope; that way the police can photocopy and fax them to others quickly, saving valuable minutes. Also include an index card that lists your child's full name and any nicknames. On the card, write down how much your child weighs and his/her height. Write down the color of his/her hair, eyes and skin. Blood type should be included. Put your child's fingerprint somewhere on the card. (Just use a stamp pad and impress his thumb and index finger.) Make a note of any birthmarks or special physical characteristics. For example, my son, Hunter, has a spider vein on his left cheek and an extremely high voice (which we're hoping changes at puberty!). My daughter Brandy has a scar on her forehead at the beginning of her hairline. Write down anything that makes your child stand out. Be specific. Everyone has things that make them unique; it could be a really nasal voice, very frizzy hair, glasses, braces, a stutter, or a certain gait. Write it all down. You'll have to update the child's age, weight and height on the card every year.

Let's say you take your kids to one of the big amusement parks that have become so popular. Take along your envelope. That way if your child gets abducted or even lost, you can give the police or security guards the index card and photos. They can immediately get that information out over the PA system, radio or cell phone. If your child is missing, you will not be thinking clearly. Chances are you will forget to mention many of the things that I suggested putting down on the card. Vague descriptions won't help the police; your cards and photos will. Carry the photos and cards with you at all times. Children are abducted everywhere, not just at large fairs, malls or amusement parks. It could be in your own driveway.

Besides prayer, prayer, and more prayer, there are practical things we can do as moms to reduce our child's chances of becoming a victim.

For more information on how to keep your child safe, log onto www.safewithin.com.

27

Some Final Thoughts

- Strive to apply God's Word in your life. Buy a Bible for yourself. Search it. I hope that this book has encouraged you to delve into the Word of God. As Christians, it is our map, so that we can survive in this crazy world.

- Accept that being a stay-at-home mother will not be easy. But you are not alone. Jesus will honor you for your decision. Remember, you are laying a strong foundation and there are no short-cuts. Stick with God's Word, pray, and know that there will be sacrifices along the way. Encourage yourself and have a good attitude. Attitude is everything. God will supply grace and mercy for you every day. Every day! You don't have to try to do this on your own.

- Your child is your finest investment. Hang in there. I promise you that you will love the interest! *It is coming!*

- Believe the Word of God and learn to recognize and ignore the lies of Satan.

- Attend a Women's Bible Study.

- This is a journey—this Christian walk. You will not be the same. Just stay on the potter's wheel. You are special to God. Know who you are in Christ Jesus! You are His child and you are a daughter of grace. This grace will cover you on the journey. It's the key.

- Know that I'm praying for you! Tackle every problem one by one with God as your helper and guide! Live out the marvelous plan He has for your life!

Angel Pattern

cut

1. Cut out angel pattern.
2. Trace pattern onto colored paper.
3. Add angelic features.
4. Write instructions on the back of each angel – as discussed in this chapter.
5. Make an envelope to store game in – or use an attractive tin.

A Devotional for Mothers

1.
Trace around a quarter to make a head.
(halo, head)

2.
Add hair

3.
Add faces.

4.
Draw a large "M" under the head.

5.
Draw arms and hands at the base of the M.

6.
Draw a bow under the arms.

7.

...ANGELS......ANGELS.........ANGELS.....ANGELS......